CAMOUFLAGE UNIFORMS

CAMOUFLAGE UNIFORMS

MARTIN J. BRAYLEY

THE CROWOOD PRESS

First published in 2009 by
The Crowood Press Ltd
Ramsbury, Marlborough
Wiltshire SN8 2HR

www.crowood.com

British Library Cataloguing-in-Publication Data
A catalogue record for this book is available from the
British Library.

ISBN 978 1 84797 137 1

Frontispiece: A US Army Signal Corps photographer pictured
wearing plain olive drab HBT fatigues that have been camouflaged
with paint. The green base has been camouflaged with what
appears to be brown, blue-grey and turquoise daubs. During the
early stages of WW11 the US Army experimented with many hand
painted camouflage designs such as the one shown.

Designed and typeset by Focus Publishing, Sevenoaks, Kent

Printed and bound in Malaysia by Konway Printhouse Sdn Bhd

Acknowledgements

I am indebted to a number of individual collectors and
interested parties for their invaluable assistance. I owe a
debt of thanks to them all for their help. Toby Brayley, for
his support and long term interest in this project, and for
donning the far from attractive 'romper suits' for photos.
John Price, for also putting pride aside and getting into a
'romper suit' for photos. Guy Cramer, CEO HyperStealth
Biotechnology Corp, for the provision of images of
company products. Ed Storey for his help with the
Canadian section and providing images. Bob Stedman for
the loan of items and his continued support. Richard
Ingram, of Sabre Sales (Southsea), for the loan of items
and long chats of a military nature. Collectors Sean
McElwain and John Bodsworth for their support and for
kindly providing photographs of uniforms from their
collections. Jaqueline Cilliers, for helping out with the
Afrikaans language. Tanya Coles, for helping out with the
Russian language. Gavin Young, Commandant, Eire
Defence Forces for providing images. Andy and Killa of
Eastwestrading Group (www.ew-trading.com) for allowing
me to photograph items from their extensive stock of
camouflage uniforms. The United States Department of
Defense, for the provision of images. Thank you all.

Contents

Introduction

'Green is... the best colour for light troops... and if put on in the spring, by autumn it nearly fades with the leaves.'

Lieutenant Colonel John Graves Simcoe,
Commanding Officer The Queen's Rangers (1777–79)

(The origins of the Queen's Rangers lay in the Seven Years War, of 1756–63. The regiment fought as scouts, or reconnaissance troops, and wore green uniforms in preference to the standard British Army scarlet. The regiment added further to its laurels during the American War of Independence when its soldiers again undertook the role of scouts.)

Definitions

Camouflage: 'protective concealment'; the art of disguising objects, troops or vehicles, so as to conceal them from detection and identification. The term 'camouflage' came into widespread use only during the Great War, undoubtedly coined from the French term *camoufler*, 'to disguise'; (the Italian term – *cammufare* – clearly has the same root). During that war, much time and effort was given to the study of the art of camouflage, particularly by the French and, to a lesser extent, by the British. Both nations formed specialist camouflage units responsible for researching and developing camouflage at all levels in the fields of warfare. However, the bulk of their attention went into devising methods of concealing military hardware such as artillery or vehicles and disguising observation posts, bunkers and similar fixed-position fortifications. Little was done in the field of individual or personal

British soldiers of the 1st Battalion Manchester Regiment, 2nd Malaya Infantry Brigade, undertake jungle training during October 1941. The men wear Khaki Drill uniform and are adding vegetation to aid in camouflage and concealment. Vegetation is an ideal camouflage medium but often needs frequent replacement as it dies off quickly.

camouflage, other, perhaps, than the work undertaken in sniper schools. Even then, the emphasis was on concealing a single individual, in a fixed position, by the use of clothing, natural materials, such as vegetation, and battle-field detritus, including tree trunks and animal carcasses.

Uniforms in a light brown 'khaki', a colour that blended with the terrain, had been in limited use with British and Indian troops since the 1840s. Although green uniforms had been used by some individual units since the seventeenth century, the use of khaki was probably the first widespread use of uniform colour for camouflage purposes. While Scarlet remained standard outside of India, the khaki uniforms adopted for use in India blended better with the dry dusty terrain. Indeed, the term itself was adopted from the Urdu and Hindi word for 'dust-coloured', and the Persian word *khak*, meaning 'dust'. By 1902 British and Commonwealth troops fighting the Boers in South Africa were dressed entirely in khaki uniforms. The British also adopted khaki for home and general service use, with scarlet uniforms being retained for dress and walking-out purposes until 1914. The term 'khaki' as a description of a colour can be confusing. In British service it applied to almost any hue, from the light tan cotton drill uniforms issued in tropical regions to the darker, brown-wool service dress, and the later green cotton uniforms, the colour of which would be better described as 'olive green', or, in US terminology, 'olive drab'.

The outbreak of the Great War saw British and Commonwealth troops dressed in khaki, while the French wore dark blue greatcoats with bright red (*Garance*) trousers and caps. This was soon changed to the universally recognized horizon blue that was still to be seen in use during the opening stages of the Second World War (Khaki had been adopted prior to the Second World War, but only for issue upon mobilization). The German states wore a variety of brightly coloured uniforms but all were soon unified, adopting field grey tunics and trousers as standard, a colour that came to typify the appearance of the German soldier of both world wars.

In 1929 the Italian Army adopted a camouflage fabric to be used on the individual issue shelter sections. The fabric was printed with a multi-colour pattern designed to break up shapes; however, on the original the patterning was highly repetitive, and it was easily discernible to the eye of any observer. This was rectified on later production fabric, and camouflage garments issued to some Italian troops during the Second World War used a modified M29 camouflage to great effect. The pattern even gained acceptance among German troops.

During the Second World War, all of the main combatant nations issued camouflage uniforms in one form or another. In 1931, the Germans had adopted the tent section 'Zeltbahn 31'. Although it was not a garment per se, it was none the less to be used as a poncho-style cover and the camouflage scheme formed the base for a variety of camouflage garments manufactured during the war.

Although the purpose of the old British monotone

khaki uniforms was camouflage, modern camouflage uniforms are generally made from fabrics having two or more base colours, thus creating a patterned camouflage. Even in the twenty-first century, however, modern armies are not entirely clad in patterned camouflage. Many, most notably Austrian and Israeli troops, still rely on monotone green or brown uniforms.

Camouflage, A Compromise

The question of individual camouflage clothing is far more complex than it may at first appear. In designing a camouflage combat uniform many factors need to be considered. The basic design requirements that make the garment suited to individual military needs, such as style and number of pockets, fabric types, and temperature ranges of intended use, are the starting point. What needs to be carried in the pockets dictates their size, and pockets are often large enough to carry at least a grenade or a weapon magazine; all too frequently, however, they are of little use to a soldier, as load-bearing equipment and body armour can prevent access. The fabric type is dictated by the requirement for a camouflage over-print, extended life, or disposability. In the past, garments were intended to have a long service life, but modern garments can have a life of as little as six months as is the case with the American ACU (Army Combat Uniform) clothing.

A Sri Lankan Air Force rank armed with an AK47 assault rifle on security patrol at a military airfield near Colombo, Sri Lanka, 2002. He wears a distinct 'urban' camouflage uniform having a sky blue base overprinted with a black, dark green and lime green colour scheme. US Department of Defense

A US Marine Corps sniper and his spotter (part of the Reconnaissance section, 26th Marine Expeditionary Unit – MEU) take aim with an M40 rifle. Both are well camouflaged courtesy of a hessian (burlap) 'scrim'-covered 'ghillie' suit. Such highly disruptive camouflage is far superior in concealing individuals than any printed camouflage, but it has seen little use with regular units and remains the domain of snipers and other specialists. US Department of Defense

The climate of the area where the clothing is intended to be used is a vital consideration. A field jacket for use in a north-western European summer would be inadequate in the winter unless provision was made for additional layers to be worn beneath it or it was provided with a thermal lining. Many nations used the layering principle, developed during the Second World War and brought to perfection by the US Army in clothing introduced from 1943. Other nations favoured separate winter and summer uniforms, notably the Warsaw Pact's Eastern European armies, although the heavy pile or similar liners were normally removable. Garments for use in hot and humid tropical jungles need to be different from those used in dry hot deserts. In deserts it can also get quite cold once the sun goes down, creating further challenges for hard-pressed designers.

Only once these design parameters had been resolved could the issues of camouflage or colour be considered. The colour of camouflage clothing is more a case of compromise than any other consideration. No single camouflage scheme will suit a soldier's every need in a given theatre, let alone provide for worldwide deployment. A typical combat patrol, even of short duration, in north-western Europe could see an infantry section moving through dense woodland, open heath, cultivated farmland and built-up urban areas. Ideally, each of these areas would have its own camouflage colour scheme for use at different times of the day and during the different seasons, but this would be wholly impractical (remembering that the quality of light at different times of the day and times of year also affects the eye's perception of colour). The compromise means taking into account the areas where camouflage would be most beneficial to the wearer, characteristically woodland and heath, and those places where it would be of less use, namely open cultivated land and urban areas.

Fabric selection is of great importance in the production of camouflage material. Historically, cotton or wool was the mainstay of military clothing. While cotton is

ACU camouflage in use with a member of the 101st Airborne Division in Iraq. This soldier is test-firing a PK-3 SMG. US Department of Defense

still used in many applications, man-made (synthetic) fibres and cotton synthetic mixes have become standard for most uniform applications. While heavyweight cotton fabric is hard-wearing it gains considerable weight when wet (and camouflage patterns also tend to darken when wet). Cotton is also slow to dry. Synthetic fibres are hard-wearing, as well as being stronger than cotton weight for weight; they also dry quickly. The type of fabric selected also has to be compatible with the application of camouflage colour. Acid dyes are compatible with Nylon fibres but Nylon tends to glow under IR light. Cotton can be readily vat dyed, but such dye tends to be excessively IR-absorbent, making the camouflage appear dark. Finding suitable colour dyes that are compatible with the fabric, as well as durable and in the required shades, is yet another problem facing designers. The US M81 woodland field jacket used 100 per cent cotton in its construction, as did the *Coat, Hot Weather, Camouflage Pattern* (RDF pattern). The DBDU, DCU and the current ACU use a 50/50 cotton Nylon mix.

Typically, the modern compromise is to provide a temperate (woodland) and arid (desert) camouflage scheme. This is typified by the British temperate DPM and desert DDPM schemes, with the temperate camouflage pattern also being used for jungle environments. The American Army has gone beyond what many would consider to be reasonable and now uses a single camouflage scheme for operations worldwide: the digital UCP (universal camouflage pattern) used on the ACU and also know as ACU camouflage, ARPAT (ARmy PATtern) or, by some (somewhat less politely), ICU!

Interestingly, identifying a nation's soldiers by their camouflage has taken a new turn in the USA. The USMC, who have always tried to stamp their particular identity into all of their uniforms and equipment (to the extent of now using different camouflage uniforms, body armour, helmets and bayonets), the US Navy, Coastguard and the

USAF all now have their own distinctive camouflage schemes; in the past, all US forces used the same nationally identifiable M81 woodland camouflage. The vast number of nations now using a NATO-type woodland camouflage (based on DPM or US M81 woodland) and using US PASGT-shape helmets, now makes it quite difficult to identify troops in the field by their uniform camouflage pattern alone.

Few nations use a dedicated snow camouflage uniform. Those that require such a scheme normally use a lightweight plain white garment that is worn over the temperate camouflage uniform. However, following the design of the German 1960s reversible white to white/green snow camouflage, some nations use a white base garment overprinted with disruptive schemes to blend in with vegetation. Only rarely is a snow-laden environment entirely white; vegetation, rocks and other terrain features will usually be present and free of snow. Italy has adopted a snow camouflage similar to the German pattern and the USMC has developed a distinct winter/snow camouflage scheme.

While manufacturers in Britain and the USA work to strict government specifications, there is still a slight degree of variation in the colours of some of the camouflage that reaches the troops. Many nations have less stringent production requirements and wide variations in the hues in a designated camouflage scheme can provide a variety of differing results. The Yugoslavian 'Lizard' and M89 patterns can be cited as a paradigm of the variety that can be encountered in a given camouflage scheme. Minor variations in the base pattern and differences in the colours used make for an interesting variety of what is essentially the same camouflage scheme. Added to these basic manu-facturers' variants are the changes to the hues that result from extended wear and fading, caused by both exposure to light and frequent washing. Making coloured dyes resistant to light and wash fading adds greatly to the cost.

A Latvian soldier fires his HK G36 rifle during a live firing practice. Diwaniyah, Iraq, 2007. He wears Latvian digital desert camouflage uniform with a US DCU helmet cover. The Latvian scheme uses somewhat large pixels in the construction of the pattern. US Department of Defense

Principles of Camouflage

In order for an object to be recognized by an observer it has to be first detected and then identified. In detection an object has to be seen to stand out from the environment in which it is placed. This detection can be because of an object's colour, shape or movement, all of which draw an observer's eye. Once detected it can then be identified. In practice, for example, a sniper scanning for targets may spot an anomaly within his arc of fire, his eye being drawn to a shape or colour not expected within the environment, or to a movement. The object then has to be identified as a valid target or a false alarm.

The process used by the observer involves the most important tool available to any soldier, the *Mk I eyeball* (human eye) and visual perception (the interpretation of images received by the eye). The human eye can process hundreds of variations in the pure colour human visual spectrum of 380–740 nanometres, and more than ten million hues. The eye is also capable of detecting the slightest movement, but it is the visual process that camouflage is best able to deceive. When viewed by the human eye, camouflage patterns are beneficial at close ranges of up to 350 metres. However, at longer ranges, colours tend to merge into a solid block of colour. In trials, movement of soldiers using camouflage-patterned uniforms was more readily observed than those wearing single-colour uniforms such as OG. It was noted that the black component of a camouflage uniform contributed greatly to observation in movement.

In military applications the deception of visual perception is achieved by the use of painted or printed camouflage (equipment and uniforms respectively). The paints and dye used need to provide camouflage in the human visual spectrum and ideally near infrared (NIR). The colours need to correspond to the surroundings, and provide highlights and shadows to produce visual depth, and the pattern has to break up shape and form and match the spatial characteristics of the background, often through mimicry. Digital patterns now appear to represent the future of camouflage uniform technology, with small blocks of colour (pixels) being used to form patterns.

Near Infrared (NIR) Imaging

Thermal imaging and near infrared imaging technologies are often confused. Thermal imaging uses the heat signature (infrared radiation) of an object; the greater the levels of radiated heat (infrared energy), the brighter the

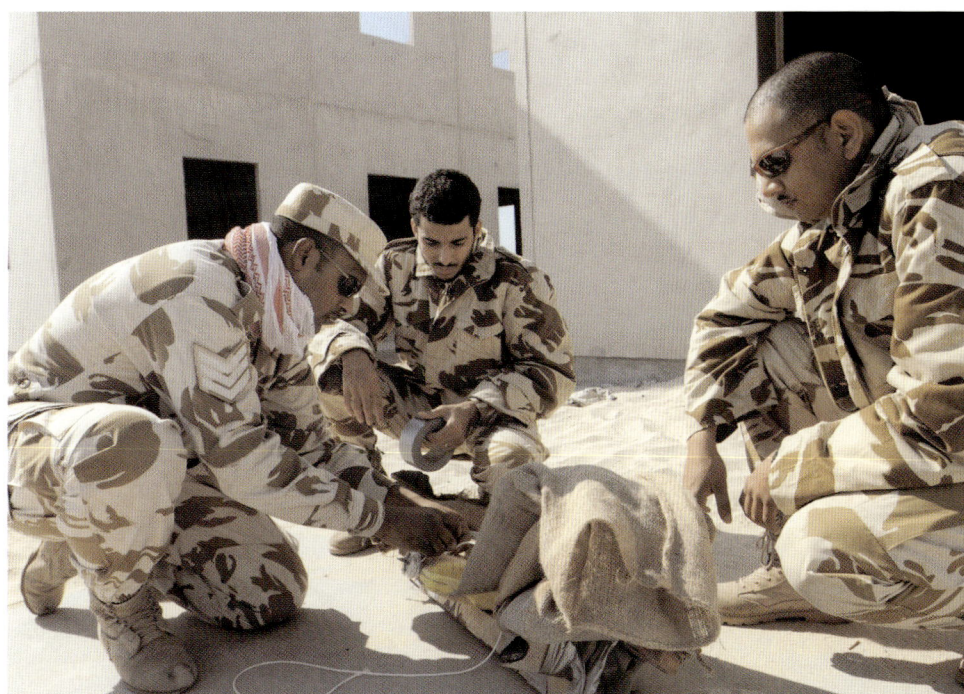

Bahrain Defence Force EOD (Explosive Ordnance Disposal) engineers examine a simulated IED (Improvised Explosive Device) during a training exercise held during January 2009. The soldiers wear a two-colour desert camouflage inspired by the British DDPM. US Department of Defense

image. Thermal imaging equipment is normally active in the temperature ranges of around -50 degrees C to 2000 degrees C. Camouflage clothing technology cannot prevent a soldier being seen by thermal imaging equipment as the human body continuously gives off heat, and it can be detected in complete darkness. Near infrared night-vision devices use light in the non-thermal near infrared wavelength, light just beyond the human visual range of the electromagnetic spectrum. NIR night-vision equipment is able to register light in the near infrared wavelength (greater than 750nm) and convert it to a visible image that can be viewed by the person using the night-vision device. The devices, frequently used as night-vision goggles (NVG), do not work in complete darkness but rely on ambient light, sunlight reflected from the moon or the small quantities of light emitted from stars. This light is in return reflected from the objects being viewed and picked up by the night-vision device. Areas can also be illuminated artificially using IR spotlights or lamps, but the IR source would be readily visible to any enemy using NVG, and easily targeted.

Normal clothing fabric and the dyes used to colour it often absorb rather than reflect IR light, so it is not normally visible to an IR night-vision device and appears dark when viewed. However, vegetation reflects IR light and therefore registers on a night-vision device as a light area; as a result, dark clothing stands out boldly against any vegetation. This problem is overcome in military camouflage clothing by using IR-reflective dyes, which make the fabrics appear as light as the surrounding vegetation when viewed through NVGs. The British DPM camouflage fabric uses a mix of IR-reflective and IR-absorbing dyes, mimicking the reflectance of vegetation and the darker natural shadows. The NIR technology used in uniform designs also make them less visible in low-light environments by reducing the reflection of ambient light. The use of IR-reflective markers added to clothing and helmets, and IR-reflective insignia has increased in recent years. The current issue US ACU jackets have IR markers on the sleeve pockets and the helmet cover, and American national flag subdued uniform patches are both IR-reflective (grey areas) and absorbing (black areas). Thus US troops readily stand out when viewed through NVGs. This is advantageous when engaging enemy troops without such markers or NVG equipment, but when the uniform is required to blend with the terrain the markers can be covered and the (velcro-attached) insignia are easily removed.

Many nations have chosen not to provide IR reflectance in their camouflage uniform fabrics. This is generally a cost-saving expedient.

A Summary of US Camouflage Clothing Development

(In a pictorial work of this kind it would be impractical to provide a definitive history of the camouflage uniforms of all nations. However, the development of US camouflage clothing is typical of worldwide advances and represents well the detail of camouflage uniform development since the Second World War.)

The Americans placed a great emphasis on the development of camouflage uniforms during the Second World War. Prior to their entry into the war, the US Army

An American Sergeant from the 29th Field Artillery Regiment, 4th Infantry Division, as viewed through NVG goggles. He wears standard UCP camouflaged ACU clothing and FLC (Fighting Load Carrier) vest with NVG goggles. Note the bold (highly IR-absorbent) 'US' at the right shoulder of the FLC vest. Iraq, January 2009. US Department of Defense

Engineer Research Board had been developing camouflage uniforms. Many variations of camouflage schemes were simply hand-painted on to HBT fatigue uniforms; the results were often garish and impractical but others formed the basis of future developments.

The *Suit, One-Piece, Jungle* was developed to provide maximum protection against insects and thorns in a jungle environment, and to provide camouflage. A modification of the plain green *Suit, Work, One-Piece, Herringbone Twill*, it was designed to be reversible from tan-dominant to green-dominant camouflage, with the tan side being the normal 'inner' side. The tan side incorporated suspenders, designed to spread the weight of the suit's cargo pocket contents, and to aid in ventilation by helping to keep the suit fabric clear of the body. It was standardized in August 1942 and is often referred to as the 'M1942 camouflage suit'. The tan (beach) camouflage used three shades of brown on a tan base while the green (jungle) side used two brown and two green shades on a lime green base. Interestingly, at least one official period document referred to the camouflage scheme as 'Frog-Skin'.

The one-piece suit was soon found to be lacking in many requirements and was declared limited standard in May 1943 when a new two-piece suit of *Jacket* and *Trousers, Herringbone Twill, Camouflage* was introduced. Despite complaints about the heavy HBT cloth, the new two-piece suit used the same camouflage fabric as had been used on the one-piece suit, as large stocks of camouflage HBT fabric were readily available. Although having the green outer and brown inner, the two-piece suit was not designed to be, nor was it normally considered reversible. The new two-piece was also issued briefly to some US troops of the 30th infantry and 2nd armoured divisions during the Normandy campaign. However, in this theatre the camouflage scheme was found to be too easily confused with the camouflage worn by German troops, with fatal consequences, and it was thus soon withdrawn. The US Marines followed the lead of the Army and introduced the *Uniform, Utility, HBT, camouflage, M1942* and later the improved *Uniform, Utility, HBT, Camouflage (modified) M1944*, both using the US Army camouflage pattern.

In 1943 a report by 1st Lieutenant Woodbury, a Quartermaster Corps observer serving in the South-West Pacific during the early part of 1943, suggested that camouflage clothing was unsuited to normal use in a jungle environment. While it was ideal for snipers, observers and troops in static positions, those wearing camouflage clothing were easier to spot when moving, and certainly more visible than men wearing clothing of a solid green colour. This had first been noted as early as October 1942, and confirmed by similar reports from the USMC. The engineer board was reluctant to accept these observations but had previously conceded that Olive Drab shade No. 7 would be the best single camouflage colour if camouflage patterns were not to be used. In March 1944 it was decided that remaining stocks of jungle camouflage fabric were to be used up but that all future orders for fabric to be used in the production of camouflage uniforms were to be of OD (Olive Drab) shade No.7, the US Army's standard colour for uniforms and equipment in all theatres.

Detail of US 4th Infantry Division and US flag patches (as worn on ACU), viewed through an IR NVG device. The flag and 4th Infantry Division patch are both grey and black when viewed by the human eye in natural daylight. Under IR light the black section of the ID patch partially reflects IR, making it appear lighter than the black sections of the flag, which fully absorb IR light, ensuring the flag stands out clearly to any observer.

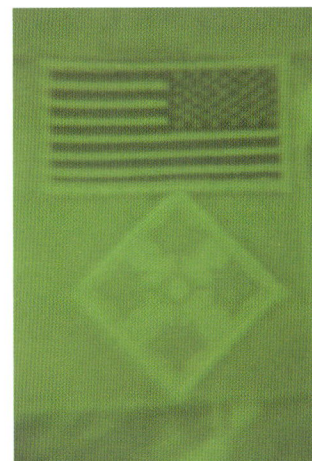

Post-Second World War Development

The United States Army Engineer Research and Development Laboratories (ERDL) experimented with camouflage in the immediate post-war years. By 1948 they had developed a scheme that was to remain on file until the 1960s. During the opening stages of the Vietnam war, US troops wore plain OG 107 (Olive Green) uniforms, with camouflaged helmet covers using the reversible brown to green 'Vine Leaf' or 'Mitchell' pattern camouflage. During 1961 the USMC experimented with the camouflaged M2 reconnaissance jacket, intended for issue to pathfinders and reconnaissance men. It is probable that no more than a few hundred of these garments were ever procured (Ref. *Project 42-58-01J*).

The need for camouflage within some units in Vietnam led to the ERDL camouflage being reassessed and provided for use in new camouflage uniforms. The new uniforms, normally referred to as the 'M65 ERDL', were first issued for evaluation during early 1966, 300 uniforms having been manufactured and despatched to Vietnam in late December 1965. During early 1967 a further 18,373 uniforms were despatched for use by reconnaissance and LRRP (long-range reconnaissance patrol) units. In June of that year ERDL was classified as standard issue for selected units. By 1969 issue was being made to regular infantry units.

ERDLE was produced in two distinct variants, the green-dominant 'Lowland' and the brown-dominant 'Highland', first issued to the USMC in 1968. The ERDL camouflage used four colours: Yellow/Green 354 (base colour), overprinted Dark Green 355, Brown 356 and Black 357. The ERDL camouflage was one of the first fully IR-treated designs. IR reflectivity was yellow/green 48 per cent, dark green 28 per cent, brown 16 per cent and black 8 per cent.

Following the end of the war in Vietnam, the US Army reverted to using plain OG 107 uniforms, although ERDL remained in use with some specialist units. A variant of the pattern was later introduced for issue to the USMC and, from 1979, units of the Rapid Deployment Force (RDF). The RDF camouflage was very similar to 'Highland' ERDL.

Continued experiments with the use of camouflage

US Vietnam period 'Mitchell' camouflage cover for the M1 helmet, showing the green side.

resulted in the introduction of the M81 'Woodland' camouflage, designed for use in Europe, but issued to US forces worldwide, Army, Navy, USMC and the USAF. The pattern was essentially an enlarged (60 per cent) version of the brown ERDL and was the base for the new Battle Dress Uniform (BDU) introduced in October 1981. M81 camouflage BDUs were still in use with some units in 2009.

The creation of the RDF brought about a new role for US forces, and a requirement for desert camouflage. In 1983 a camouflage scheme that had been developed during the early 1970s was introduced for use with the new Desert Battle Dress Uniform (DBDU). The six-colour camouflage used a base of two tones of light tan and two of red brown, overprinted with small black and white spots or 'chips', giving rise to the moniker 'Chocolate Chip'. The DBDU saw use in the Gulf War in 1990 although by this time a replacement for the DBDU had already been found. The Desert Combat Uniform (DCU) used a tri-colour camouflage consisting of a base of Tan 492 overprinted with large areas of Khaki 494 and smaller shadows of Brown 493. The camouflage was under production in 1990 but was not issued prior to the end of the Gulf War. The new uniform camouflage made it cooler in use, as it had been found that the excessive dark areas of the DBDU tended to absorb heat from the sun.

The move to a new family of twenty-first-century camouflage patterns was instigated by the USMC. During the development of the USMC camouflage, more than sixty commercial and military patterns were evaluated by the US Army Natick Soldier Systems Center. One of the leading patterns in the trial was the Candian CADPAT camouflage scheme, a digital pattern print. From the patterns examined, the Marines produced a digital camouflage design – MARPAT (MARine PATtern) – in three distinct colour variants suited to woodland, urban and desert environments. The urban design was dropped but the woodland and desert patterns were introduced into service in 2002. Woodland MARPAT camouflage uses dye colours Green 474, Khaki 475, Coyote 476 and Black 477. (Interestingly, the US Army made a point of discarding black in its later UCP camouflage.) The Marines Desert MARPAT scheme uses four colours: Urban Tan 478; Desert Light Tan 479; Urban Light Grey 480, and Light Coyote 481. The old M81 'Woodland' and DCU 'Desert'

camouflage uniforms were declared obsolete in USMC service by 2006.

The USMC camouflage was patented under United States Patent 6805957. A summary of the patent reads as follows:

> The system provides camouflage in both the human visible light and the near infrared range. The system depends on macro pattern resulting from a repeat of a micro pattern. The coloring used includes at least four colorings from dyes that in combination produce a percent reflectance value comparable to that of the negative space of the camouflaged subject's surroundings. The system functions by a macro pattern being disruptive of the subject's shape and a micro pattern having sharp edge units of a size capable of blending the subject into its background. The relative lightness values and percentages of total pattern, wet or dry, are sufficient to produce a percent reflectance of acceptable colors, in terms of lightness values unlike current four-color camouflage.

The US Army followed hot on the heels of the USMC with regard to digital camouflage, introducing the UCP (universal camouflage pattern) used on the Army Combat Uniform (ACU). The UCP was a direct development of MARPAT. Introduced in June 2004, it is a three-colour digital camouflage consisting of a base of Sand 500 overprinted with Light Warrior Grey 501 and Grey 502. A set of jacket and trousers cost $88 at the time of first fielding the new garments; the old BDU had been somewhat cheaper, at $56.

The UCP seems to have taken camouflage to a new and alternative level. However, the requirement to provide light and dark areas in camouflage patterns, to replicate natural shadow and highlight, seems to have been disregarded by the US Army. It decided to leave black out of the scheme, explaining its decision in the following official comment:

> Technological advances have provided engineers with better data analysis. Black was originally put in the BDU to separate the other colors and to help with shadows. What was found is no matter what color you make a uniform, if black is a property, and you are not standing in front of something black, the moment you move, the eye immediately picks up the black. Testing found that a digitized pattern worked better in more environments.

The universally accepted minimum requirement for a distinct and separate woodland and desert pattern of camouflage has also been disregarded, with UCP being designated for use in all theatres and all terrain. This one-scheme approach has undoubtedly compromised the effectiveness of individual concealment in different terrains but the cost-saving implications of one pattern have perhaps outweighed these factors.

During the trials related to developing a new camouflage for the proposed ACU, a number of patterns were considered. Crye Precision submitted 'Multicam', which was field-tested during 2003/4. Highly regarded, it was none the less discarded in favour of the UCP.

Africa

RIGHT: French-manufacture camouflage jacket used by the army of the Togolese Republic. The style of jacket is copied from the French F1 but uses the old 'Lizard' pattern camouflage. As well as Togo, this jacket type is also used by the Republic of Mali armed forces. It is labelled 'Veste F1'.

LEFT: A Malian soldier of the Economic Community Military Observation Group (ECOMOG) awaits departure for Liberia in support of Operation *Assured Lift*. He wears the French F1-style 'Lizard' camouflage jacket. US Department of Defense

May 2007: Rwandan Defence Force soldiers await air transport from a Rwanda air base to Sudan to aid in peacekeeping in the Darfur region of Sudan. Their desert camouflage uniforms use the US 'Choc-Chip' camouflage as a design base but with richer hues, and an added earth brown colour. US Department of Defense

A Nigerian soldier of the ECOMOG providing airfield security for a United States Air Force C-130E offloading Malian troops at a Liberian base. He wears a woodland camouflage uniform with an unmistakeably British-style 'stable belt'. US Department of Defense

2006: soldiers of the Cameroon Army parade wearing a camouflage uniform inspired by the French 'Lizard' pattern.

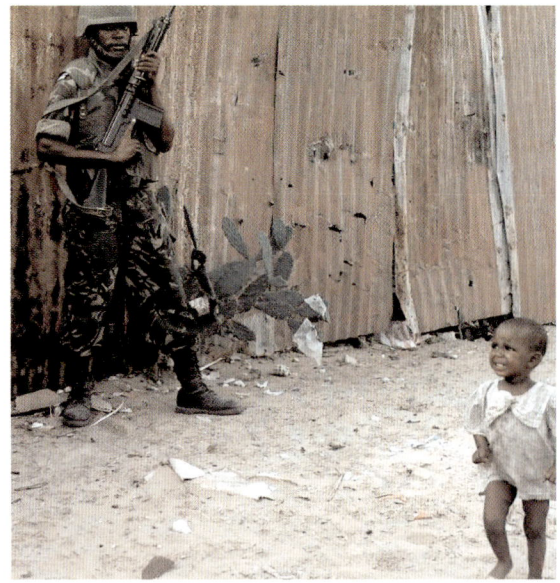

A soldier of the Botswana Defence Force photographed during an arms raid on the Bakara Market, Somalia, as a part of Operation *Restore Hope*. The young Somali child appears suitably intimidated.
US Department of Defense

ABOVE: Troops of the 5th Ghanaian Battalion (GHANBATT 5) parade in Ghana after returning from their deployment to Sierra Leone as a part of the UN peacekeeping training mission Operation *Focus Relief*. US Department of Defense

RIGHT: Armed with an H&K G3A3 rifle, this Kenyan soldier was photographed while taking part in Exercise *Natural Fire* during August 2006. He wears a camouflage jacket in British DPM and a shirt of the same camouflage material.
US Department of Defense

ABOVE: Uniform shirt as worn by the Afrikaner Weerstandsbeweging (Afrikaner Resistance Movement), formed in 1973 by Eugène Terre'Blanche to promote the formation of an independent Boerestaat for Boerevolk in the old Zuid-Afrikaansche Republiek (South African Republic) and the Oranje Vrystaat (Republic of the Orange Free State). The camouflage uniform was worn with a maroon beret. Photo courtesy J. Bodsworth

ABOVE RIGHT: Bophuthatswana was the South African Bantusan (homeland) of the Setswana-speaking peoples, existing between 1977 and 1994. In 1994 the Bantusan were all forcibly incorporated into the new post-apartheid South Africa, not without some bloodshed. The camouflage is based upon the British DPM, the garment being made by ActionFit in 1993.

FAR RIGHT: Transkei ('the area beyond the Kei River') was one of the South African autonomous Bantusan (homelands). Along with Ciskei it was peopled by tribes speaking the Xhosa language. Transkci was in existence from 1976 until 1994 during which time they procured their own camouflage uniforms. This example was made by DUX Uniforms (Pty) Ltd.

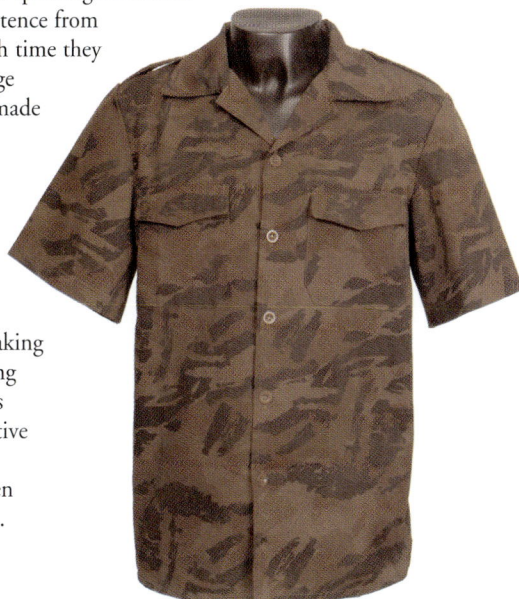

RIGHT: Although separate from Transkei, Ciskei ('on this side of the Kei River') was the second Bantusan (homeland) of the Xhosa-speaking people of South Africa, existing between 1981 and 1994. This Ciskei shirt has a quite repetitive camouflage with dull and indistinct hues of brown, green and charcoal on a brown base. It was made by Standfast.

LEFT: The South African Police (SAP) introduced their own pattern of camouflage in 1968. This shirt uses the second design camouflage dating to 1976. The police patterns have now generally been replaced by the 'Soldier 2000' camouflage but are retained by a few specialist units. This shirt was made by Endeavour (Sic) in 1986.

The Republic of South African flag worn on the left sleeve of the 'Soldier 2000' uniform.

RIGHT: South African National Defence Force camouflage, introduced during the mid-1990s. It is often referred to as the '2000' pattern camouflage, after its use in the 'Soldier 2000' combat clothing system. This jacket was made by FIELDS WEAR in 1999 and is named to Sersant (the Afrikaans for Sergeant) Jali. The manufacturer's label includes the notification 'State Property. Not For Sale'.

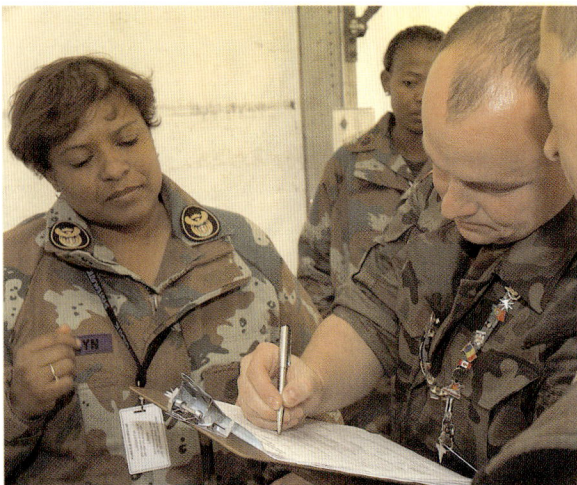

LEFT: South African army Adjutant-Offisier (Warrant Officer 1st Class) Lucricia Koayn (left) assists Polish Major Mariusz Michalski during a communications exercise held in Germany during 2007. WO Koayn wears the current issue South African 'Soldier 2000' camouflage uniform.

ABOVE: Camouflage shirt worn by members of the South-West Africa People's Organization. SWAPO was formed to gain independence from South Africa, which was granted to Namibia in 1990. Photo courtesy J. Bodsworth

ABOVE RIGHT: Namibian camouflage shirt, based on the British DPM camouflage scheme but using a highly subdued print.

RIGHT: Namibian camouflage shirt. One of a number of variants that can be encountered in use with Namibian forces, this example was produced in Bophuthatswana during 1992. Photo courtesy J. Bodsworth

Label from Namibian camouflage shirt, showing it was made in Bophuthatswana in 1992. Photo courtesy J. Bodsworth

Australia

RIGHT: A Corporal from the Royal Australian Army's 7th Signals has a shave in the field using the wing mirror of a Land Rover. He wears the standard Aussie DPCU uniform and boonie hat.

BELOW: Australian DPC (disruptive pattern camouflage) as used on the DPCU (disruptive pattern camouflage uniform), commonly referred to as 'Auscam'. Introduced in the mid-1980s, 'Auscam' uses a tan base overprinted with patches of charcoal, medium green, brown and red/brown. This camouflage is used with Australian dress orders 4A *Barrack Dress DPCU* and 4B *Field Dress DPCU*. This shirt is dated 1990.

ABOVE: Although rain garments are essentially outside of the scope of this work, some mention is warranted. Most nations produce rain garments in the same camouflage as standard field wear, although a few countries are known to use camouflage schemes that are unique to rainwear. During the Vietnam War this camouflage raincoat was produced for Aussie troops, at a time when their field uniform was plain OG. Often called the 'Can't see me' coat, it provided a serviceable waterproof garment during the wet season. This item was made in 1971 by the Oxford Clothing Co.

ABOVE: Australian SAS wings fitted to the right shoulder of the DPCU shirt.

RIGHT: The post-2002 third pattern DPDU (disruptive pattern desert uniform) camouflage shirt. Collectors acknowledge three camouflage schemes for Australian desert pattern garments. The first pattern was a three-colour camouflage, while the second and third patterns were almost identical, but for a distinct yellow hue to the tan base of the third pattern.

BELOW: Australian troops serving with ISAF (International Security Assistance Force) in Afghanistan cross a river, accompanied by local children. The men wear the third pattern DPDU and carry Steyr AUG rifles. NATO

Austria

RIGHT: The Austrian M57 camouflage was based on Second World War German designs and is very similar to patterns used by the SS. It had a distinctly pink base overprinted with two tones of green and two of brown. Camouflage uniforms were relegated to reservist use in 1978 following the issue of the plain Olive Drab (OD) *Feldanzug 75* (field uniform 75) and are no longer in service.

BELOW: The Austrians are among the few armed forces that in modern times have deemed that a single colour uniform, rather than a multi-colour camouflage, is best suited to their military requirements. However, as can be seen here, the camouflage cover for the French F2 Spectra helmet has seen use with Austrian troops on their M92 helmet. The standard helmet cover, and uniform, are a plain OD. Austrian troops are also known to have used US tri-colour DCU uniforms. US Department of Defense

Belgium

ABOVE: During the Korean War members of the Belgian Battalion catch up on the news from home during their deployment at Waegwan. The men wear the early-style Belgian camouflage smock, with half zip, based on the British Denison and using a similar camouflage pattern. USNA

ABOVE: 1956-made Belgian smock, again inspired by the British Second World War Denison. It uses the M54 'Brushstroke' camouflage pattern that replaced the Denison scheme and that was itself soon replaced by the 'Jigsaw' camouflage. The pocket flaps of this garment are secured using buttons, a modification introduced in 1956; earlier smocks used press snaps.

ABOVE: Manufacturer's label from the 'Brushstroke' camouflage smock, showing the year of production (1956), size, and 'ABL' for Armée Belge-Belgisher Leger (French/Flemish Belgian Army).

LEFT: The original version of Belgian 'Jigsaw' camouflage, developed during the 1950s. This smock, of a similar style to the earlier 'Brushstroke' pattern smock, is fitted with its detachable hood and is dated 1958.

ABOVE: Wearing standard 'Jigsaw' camouflage, Belgian Adjutant (Warrant Officer) Kurt Declercq moves cautiously forward during a NATO exercise. He is followed by a US soldier wearing M81 'Woodland' camouflage. US Department of Defense

ABOVE: The third version of the Belgian 'Jigsaw' camouflage. The pattern had evolved since the 1950s original, as had the now quite distinctive colours. It bears the Belgian flag on the left sleeve (RIGHT).

RIGHT: Belgian 'Flecktarn' camouflage. Based on the Bundeswehr camouflage, the Belgian version was used by the Air Commando and ground units of the Luchtmacht (air force). This jacket is dated 1989.

BELOW: A Belgian Armed Forces Luchtcomponent (air component) ground crewman marshals an F-16 during an air combat exercise held in Jordan, 2007. The airman wears Belgian desert camouflage T-shirt and trousers.

Bulgaria

LEFT: Bulgarian 1953 splinter-pattern camouflage. The camouflage used for this one-piece suit was inspired by German wartime patterns. This example is somewhat faded; base colours can vary from brown to grey and they were normally somewhat crudely printed. One-piece suits, dismissed by Britain and the US during the Second World War, remained popular with Eastern Bloc nations well into the 1990s. A similar garment was also produced using the raindrop-pattern camouflage based on that briefly used by Poland and, later, the DDR. The breast and rear seat pockets are compartmentalized and allow carriage of three Russian PPsH 41 magazines in each pocket; this was the standard Bulgarian infantry weapon during the 1950s until eventually replaced by the ubiquitous Kalashnikov.

ABOVE: A 1961 splinter-pattern camouflage jacket as used by Bulgarian paratroopers and special forces. This winter jacket, issued with a detachable liner with faux fur collar, was made in 1964. At this time only selected troops and units were equipped with camouflage uniforms.

LEFT: The last (1991) splinter-pattern camouflage scheme, which had evolved from the original M1953 pattern, but differed in pattern detail and colour, and was noticeably different from the scheme used on the 1960s paratrooper jacket; there is a clearly defined space around each section of brown and green, with no overlap. Following the fall of the Warsaw Pact, camouflage uniforms were introduced for all Bulgarian troops.

RIGHT: 2004: Bulgarian Army soldiers prepare to enter a building for room-clearance training during an urban warfare exercise. The men wear the late-pattern splinter-camouflage uniforms. US Department of Defense

LEFT: The three-colour 'Frog-Skin' camouflage coverall was introduced during the early 1970s, intended for use by specialist units such as paratroopers and border guards. The camouflage pattern uses a grey base overprinted with green blotches and a red/brown raindrop pattern. The green blotches are individual spots or larger clumps. From any viewing distance other than close-up, the camouflage appears as green patches on grey. As with the 1953 suit, the pockets of this coverall are compartmentalized to carry the magazines of the 7.62mm AKK assault rifle.

ABOVE: Bulgarian five-colour woodland camouflage shirt introduced in 2003. The woodland camouflage has now replaced the older splinter pattern garments in Bulgarian service. This garment was made in 2006.

RIGHT: Bulgarian paratrooper Leitenant (2nd Lieutenant) Rumen Lozanov of the 1st Special Forces Battalion 68th Special Forces Brigade, Bulgarian Army. April 2008. US Department of Defense

LEFT: Desert camouflage uniform in stone base colour overprinted with irregular patches of very light green and medium brown. Made in 2006, the shirt carries the standard factory-applied Bulgarian Armed Forces national insignia.

Canada

ABOVE LEFT: *Smock, Parachutist, Disruptive Pattern.* The 'Para smock' was issued to Canadian airborne units between 1968 and 1995, earlier plain OD patterns soon being replaced by DPM. The Canadian Airborne Regiment was formed in 1968 to provide a rapid reaction force. It was disbanded in 1995 after an unfortunate event that had taken place during the regiment's service in Somalia during 1993.

ABOVE: Canadian DPM smock as trialled during the mid-1970s. Similar to the plain green OG107 combat uniform, this pattern was allotted Canadian NSN (NATO Stock Numbers) and was even promulgated in some equipment catalogues suggesting that it was almost authorized for issue but then cancelled. Most of the production run was sold to Tanzania (Canada was training their army at the time) and some were sold as surplus. Image courtesy Ed Storey

LEFT: Variant of DPM camouflage produced for trials during the 1980s. This pattern was provided to the Canadian 4th Brigade, serving in Germany, for field trials, but it was not adopted for general issue. Image courtesy Ed Storey

RIGHT: An unusual pattern of camouflage developed for trials in the early 80s but not adopted. It is shown worn with the experimental 1982-pattern web equipment pistol set. This camouflage pattern was seriously considered for adoption by Canadian forces but was discarded. Image courtesy Ed Storey

RIGHT: The upper left sleeve of the CADPAT shirt has a large velcro patch covered by a fabric flap with a smaller section of velcro fitted to it. The smaller outer velcro patch is for the attachment of the national flag, the larger section beneath the flap is used for the fitting of a brassard, which would otherwise require an epaulette loop at the shoulder. A subdued flag is worn overseas and a coloured flag within Canada, the flag not being worn is fitted below the flap. Image courtesy Ed Storey

LEFT: Typical bilingual Canadian Department of Defence garment label as found in CADPAT jackets.

ABOVE: *Coat, Combat, Lightweight CADPAT* (CADPAT – CAnadian PATtern). The second-pattern shirt, with concealed buttons and added refinements, which had been developed as a result of intensive troop user trials prior to the introduction of the CADPAT clothing and equipment system. Many soldiers had asked for the lower pockets to be deleted so the shirt could be comfortably worn tucked into the trousers but it was decided that the pockets should be retained.

RIGHT: *Man's: Jacket, Garrison Dress, Land.* The garrison jacket was a short-lived item, which, as the name suggests, and despite the camouflage, was used only for garrison (barrack) dress and not field use. Introduced in 1989, it was soon deemed a superfluous item and its use was discontinued in 1994.

LEFT: 'CANADA' shoulder title, insignia of the 1st Canadian Mechanised Brigade Group (1 CMBG), and 'Corporal' chevrons worn on the right sleeve of the garrison jacket. The Canadian flag was not worn on the garrison jacket.

LEFT: First-pattern CADPAT arid uniform referred to as the ARPAT (ARrid PATtern) and used by Canadian forces in Afghanistan. This tunic is manufactured in the same style as the temperate CADPAT. Image courtesy Ed Storey

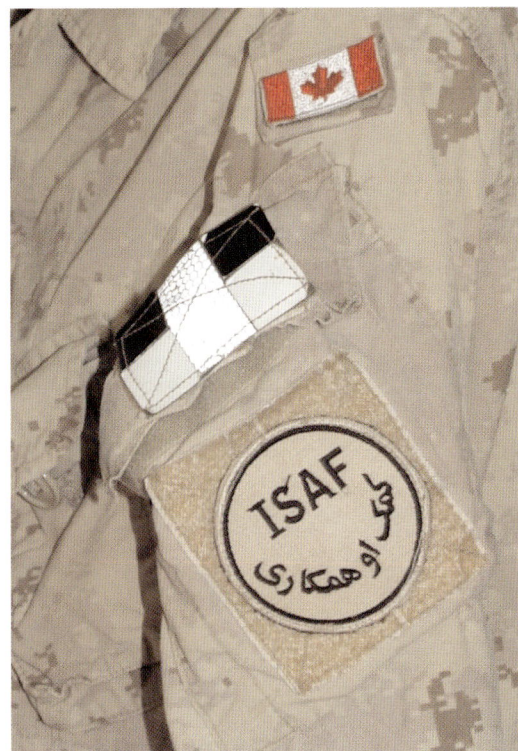

ABOVE: Second-pattern ARPAT uniform, showing detail of the insignia and pocket arrangement on the left sleeve. This garment was worn by Master Corporal Moreau when he served with ISAF. Image courtesy Ed Storey

RIGHT: The second-pattern arid version of the ARPAT uniform in use with Canadian troops serving in Kandahar with ISAF Afghanistan. This jacket was similar to the original pattern but had additional sleeve pockets on the upper sleeves, similar to the arrangement on the US ACU jacket. ISAF

Central Asia

RIGHT: Kazakhstan Army woodland jacket 2007. It bears rank epaulettes with a single star over two bars, indicating a Major. The right breast bears a name tape 'KAZAKSTAN', with the wearer's blood group worn on the left in Russian style.

LEFT: Kazakhstan Army sleeve insignia, showing the national eagle and sun device.

LEFT: A Kazakhstan Senior Lieutenant wears the red/brown-based three-colour camouflage uniform. His sleeve emblem reads 'KAZAKSTAN'; interestingly, Kazakh national insignia can be found to read both 'Kazakhstan' or 'Kazakstan'. US Department of Defense

A Kazakh soldier on a field training exercise. He wears the same uniform as the colour party Lieutenant, with a camouflage helmet cover. US Department of Defense

A Kazakh paratrooper sergeant in parade dress. He wears the woodland camouflage jacket with a typically Soviet-style airborne forces blue beret. US Department of Defense

LEFT: Russian-made Kazakhstani six-colour desert camouflage version of the US DBDU camouflage. Photo courtesy Sean McElwain

RIGHT: Kazakhstan EOD soldiers working to clear abandoned munitions in Iraq during 2005. The soldier in the foreground wears a Russian KLMK coverall with an armoured vest and helmet cover (over a US PASGT helmet) of Kazakh six-colour desert camouflage. The soldier to the rear wears a uniform of the same camouflage scheme, based on the American 'Choc-Chip' DBDU camouflage. The US DBDU was used by Kazakh forces in Iraq prior to the introduction of the Kazakh scheme. US Department of Defense

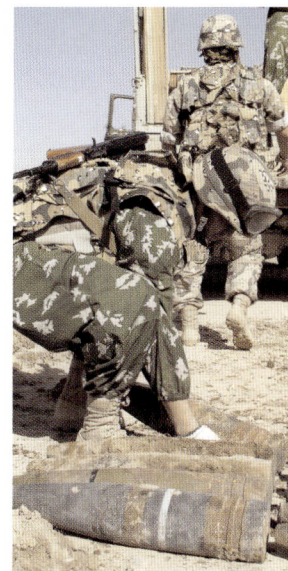

RIGHT: Diwaniyah, Iraq, 2006. A Kazakh soldier wears the Kazakh desert camouflage uniform with a US M81 woodland camouflage fragmentation vest and US PASGT helmet. US Department of Defense

ABOVE: Azerbaijan Army soldiers parade during a review of CENTRASBAT (Central Asian Peacekeeping Battalion). CENTRASBAT was formed in 1995 from Kazakhstan, Kyrgystan and Uzbekistan units to provide a regional security battalion. The soldiers wear Turkish woodland camouflage uniforms. US Department of Defense

ABOVE: Uzbekistan camouflage blouson jacket badged to a Kichik Leytnant (Lieutenant 2nd class). The camouflage scheme uses a tan base with a light brown and lime green overprint. Photo courtesy Sean McElwain

LEFT: Uzbekistan airborne troops wearing a camouflage uniform similar to the Russian-inspired red/brown base uniform worn by Kazak forces. The sleeve patch reads 'OZBEKISTON'. US Department of Defense

China
People's Republic of China, Republic of China (Taiwan)

LEFT: The Type 99 woodland camouflage jacket. The pattern is inspired by the US M81 woodland camouflage. This jacket is made in the blouson style which is very popular in Chinese service. Garment courtesy Eastwestrading

ABOVE: People's Liberation Army (PLA) armoured troops at Shenyang training base in China, 2007. All wear the Type 99 woodland camouflage uniform. US Department of Defense

ABOVE: Chinese People's Liberation Army (Navy) uniform blouson jacket issued to Marines. It uses a sky blue base camouflage overprinted with a medium and dark blue camouflage scheme. It bears the two-star rank epaulettes of a Zhong Wei (Lieutenant junior grade, or Sub-Lieutenant). The left sleeve has two small loops, which are used for the attachment of unit insignia fitted with small velcro tabs.

LEFT: The Type 03 camouflage, also known as 'Highlands' or 'Tibetan Flecktarn'. This camouflage was used by PLA troops serving in Tibet and other mountainous areas. The jacket is of a much heavier fabrication than most Chinese uniforms but still lacks the typically high-quality production of European- or US-manufacture uniform.

ABOVE: Zhanjiang, November 2006. Somewhat wet and grubby Commandos of the Chinese Marines, 1st Marine Brigade PLA(N). The men, armed with the Type 97 assault rifle, wear the blue navy camouflage uniform. US Department of Defense

ABOVE: PLA 07 pattern woodland digital camouflage. This is the first pattern of uniform with epaulette (shoulder) straps for rank. Later manufacture garments display collar rank and are not fitted with epaulette straps. This jacket bears the Chinese flag on the left sleeve and has two loops stitched to the right sleeve for the fitting of unit insignia.

ABOVE: PLA special forces 'Tigerstripe' camouflage uniform, one of many new-generation uniforms introduced into the Chinese forces over the past decade. The shoulders show the rank of Shao Wei (2nd Lieutenant). This garment is dated 2007.

LEFT: PLA special forces insignia fitted to the left sleeve of the 'Tigerstripe' jacket.

RIGHT: Taiwanese 'Tigerstripe' camouflage shirt. It bears the post 1981 rank insignia of a Chung Shih (Sergeant). The 'Tigerstripe' camouflage was first used by the ARVN (Army of the Republic of Vietnam) and became synonymous with US army advisers during the early 1960s.

31

Croatia

RIGHT: Croatian woodland camouflage tunic, bearing the Hrvatska Vojska (Croatia Army) tape above the left breast and the standard HV army insignia on the left sleeve. The right sleeve bears the unit insignia of the Imotski 115 Brigada. The HV were formed in 1991 following the Croatian break-away from Yugoslavia.

Detail of Croatian 115th Brigade insignia worn on the right sleeve.

Artillerymen of the 2nd Guards Brigade, Croatian Army, fire a 122mm Howitzer during field firing exercises.

Czechoslovakia
(Czech Republic, Slovakia)

RIGHT: The Vz95 was the first new camouflage scheme of the Czech Republic, formed along with Slovakia following the division of Czechoslovakia into two nations in 1993. The new woodland camouflage scheme was aimed at distancing the fledgling nation from its Warsaw Pact roots and providing a camouflage similar to the woodland schemes used within NATO. The Czech Republic was accepted into NATO in 1999. This parka-style jacket was one of the first garments manufactured in the new camouflage scheme.

ABOVE: Vz60 'Mlok' ('Salamander') camouflage used by Czech forces during the 1960s. Normally associated with airborne and special forces units, it was also used by regular troops. This winter jacket is dated 1961.

RIGHT: Vz60 'Jehlici' ('Needles') camouflage. This camouflage is a brown raindrop-type scheme printed over a grey/brown base with sage green spots. The Vz60 camouflage schemes were replaced by the plain green Vz85 scheme in 1985. This garment is dated 1962.

RIGHT: Czech Republic flash and early pattern large national flag worn on the left sleeve of the Vz95 camouflage jacket.

LEFT: This four-colour desert-type camouflage has yet to be identified positively, with few collectors agreeing on its definitive origin. As well as the jacket and trousers, a boonie hat, baseball cap, boots and drawstring carry bag are also found in this camouflage scheme. It was undoubtedly of Czech manufacture and was possibly intended for use by the Czech military but not adopted.

RIGHT: Major Frantisek Okrzesa of the Czech Republic army. He wears a Vz95 camouflage jacket with small pattern national flag on the left sleeve pocket. US Department of Defense

LEFT: Czech Republic desert parka, bearing the insignia of the 4th Rapid Deployment Brigade, the Czech airborne brigade, established in 1994. This parka, dated 2006, is typical of the fuller-length garments long favoured by Czech and Eastern European forces, although standard-length jackets are also issued. The Czech Republic flash is worn on the left shoulder, above a small version of the national flag.

ABOVE RIGHT: Slovakian army engineers of the Multinational Division Central South (MND-CS) wear two-tone brown on tan Slovakian desert camouflage, Iraq, 2006. On the left sleeve is the title 'SLOVAKIA' over the Slovak double cross (Cross of Lorraine) patch. The ballistic vests are American woodland pattern camouflage. US Department of Defense

LEFT: Detail of the insignia of the 4th Rapid Deployment Brigade, worn on the right sleeve of the desert parka.

RIGHT: Slovakian woodland pattern camouflage coat. The design is influenced by the US M81 woodland pattern but has a distinct pattern. Photo courtesy Sean McElwain

ABOVE: US Marines 'cam up' Slovakian troops during a joint US/Slovak exercise held in the USA during 1996. The Slovakian troops wear woodland pattern camouflage with a subdued Slovak cross emblem printed in outline on the left sleeve pocket. US Department of Defense

Denmark

RIGHT: Danish camouflage jacket using the M84 black and green on tan 'Pletsløring' (spot camouflage) scheme. Similar to the German 'Flecktarn', this scheme was also used by Latvian, Lithuanian and Estonian forces serving with SFOR (Stabilization Force).

ABOVE: A Danish dog handler photographed with his German Shepherd dog. The handler and dog provide perimeter patrols for Karup Air Station. He wears an M84 camouflage jacket and trousers. The trousers have an interesting light-green-dominant camouflage rather than the normal dark-green-dominant scheme used on the jacket. US Department of Defense

RIGHT: Troops from Multinational Division – Central South (MND-CS), Iraq. Left to right are US Army Lieutenant Colonel Patrick wearing the ACU uniform, Danish Army Captain Gottlieb with the M1999 'Ørken' (desert) three-colour camouflage uniform, and an Iraqi Border Police officer wearing a woodland-style camouflage. US Department of Defense

East Germany

RIGHT: 'Flächentarn' (patterned camouflage), also commonly referred to as 'Blumentarn' (flower camouflage). (NVA documents refer to this camouflage as 'Flächendruck', or pattern print). It has a grey base overprinted with brown and two shades of turquoise green. Introduced into the NVA (National Volksarmee) in 1958, it continued in production until 1967. 'Flächentarn' was the earliest camouflage pattern provided on general issue. Ammunition pouches, e-tool covers and packs (as well as helmet covers, kitbags, shelter sections and other items) were also produced in this camouflage scheme. It was the earliest use of camouflage for such ancillary items, which is now a widespread practice.

LEFT: The 'Flächentarn' uniform in use with an NVA mortar team during the early 1960s. The uniform jacket was the first to have sleeve pockets that could easily be accessed when wearing load bearing equipment.

LEFT: 'Strichtarn' (raindrop or needle pattern camouflage). NVA troops nicknamed this scheme *Ein-strich-kein-strich*, or 'one streak no streak'. The camouflage uses a grey/brown base overprinted with small brown stripes and was copied from the Polish raindrop pattern. 'Strichtarn' was introduced under NVA order number 2/65 of May 1965, with issue not being completed until the end of 1969. As with the 'Flächentarn', many ancilliary items were produced in this camouflage scheme.

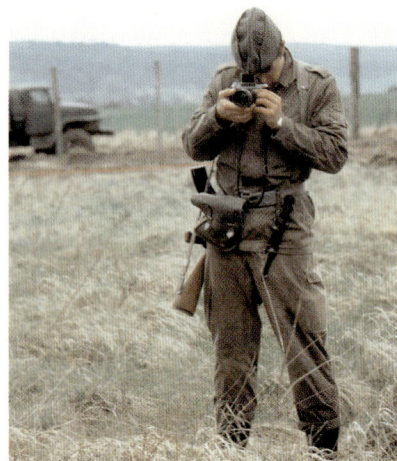

An NVA Unterfeldwebel (Sergeant) photographs NATO troops monitoring the border between East and West Germany. He wears the 'Strichtarn' summer uniform with matching camouflage MPiK 7.62mm ammunition pouch. US Department of Defense

ABOVE: Egypt 1983. Egyptian paratroopers armed with AKMS rifles form a defensive perimeter. They wear locally designed and produced desert 'rock' camouflage uniforms. US Department of Defense

ABOVE: An Egyptian soldier undertaking small-arms training at Mubarak Military City, Egypt, listens to a briefing prior to a range practice. His camouflage uniform has a tan-dominant base with green, black and brown print. His helmet is covered with a matching cover. US Department of Defense

LEFT: Egyptian desert camouflage shirt using a tan-dominant base with green, black and brown print. The scheme can also be found in a brown-dominant print that does not include green. Photo courtesy Sean McElwain

ABOVE: Irish Ceannaire (Corporal) wearing the IDF camouflage uniform and armed with the Austrian Steyr AUG assault rifle. This camouflage is commonly referred to as 'Paddyflage' by collectors. Courtesy Irish Defence Forces

ABOVE: Óglaigh na hÉireann (Irish Defence Forces) camouflage jacket. This style of camouflage was first issued in limited quantity to overseas contingents during 1999. The item illustrated is a well-designed jacket, based on the British *Smock, Combat, Windproof, Arctic*. It was made in 1999 by Portwest Ltd. Garments are also made by Seyntex.

RIGHT: A further view of the Óglaigh na hÉireann IDF camouflage. The new camouflage replaced the plain green uniform that had previously been worn, although British DPM had seen limited service with Irish forces. Courtesy Irish Defence Forces

Finland

ABOVE: Finnish United Nations troops wearing M62 camouflage uniforms shortly after arrival at Grootfontein Logistics Base from where they deployed as peacekeepers in Namibia. US Department of Defense

ABOVE: A Vääpeli (Warrant Officer) of the signals branch (shown by the insignia worn on the left-sleeve velcro patch) wearing the Finnish army digital M05 camouflage jacket. US Department of Defense

ABOVE: Plain white snow camouflage reverse of the M62 jacket The pockets' arrangements are mirrored, having a single breast pocket top left and a single hip pocket lower right on both the snow and three-colour sides of the jacket.

ABOVE: The M1962 camouflage. The jacket is fully reversible. Shown here is the three-colour temperate camouflage, reversing to plain white.

ABOVE: The latest camouflage issued to Finnish troops is the digital pattern M05. The colours used in the M05 can be traced to those of the M91 camo, which in turn used similar colours to the M62. This jacket was made by Seyntex in 2007.

LEFT: The M91 camouflage that replaced the M62 pattern. This jacket is badged to the Suomen Kansainvälinen Valmiusjoukk (Finnish Rapid Deployment Force) that deployed to Kosovo in 1999. The right sleeve bears the 'KFOR' (Kosovo FORce) patch.

France

ABOVE: During the Six-Day War of 1967 Israeli soldiers wear a mix of plain OD (Olive Drab) and French 'Lizard' camouflage. The soldier at left wears camouflage trousers with OD jacket and the soldier at right OD trousers with camouflage jacket.

RIGHT: 'Lizard' pattern camouflage adopted in 1953 and used extensively in Algeria. During the 1960s the pattern saw only limited use by French troops, mainly the Foreign Legion, but it was adopted by many former colonies and other nations. This early production jacket was made by J. Pauwells & Cie Merville. Many of these jackets were later used by Israeli forces.

LEFT: Prior to the start of the first Gulf War, French troops were wearing the plain OD F1 uniform. The OD F1 uniform was worn by the first French troops to arrive in the Gulf theatre in 1990 under Opération Daguet, the code name for the French involvement in the Gulf. The name was popularly applied to the camouflaged desert uniform issued in that theatre. Although the new 'Daguet' desert camouflage was authorized in 1989 and issued for the Gulf conflict, the old OD F1 was still much in evidence at the close of the war. This example of French desert camouflage was fabricated in the same cut as the standard OD F1 jacket and was made in 1990. Production later mirrored the F2 jacket, losing the skirt pockets.

Djibouti, 2006. A French Caporal (Lance-Corporal) desert-survival instructor addresses a platoon of students at the Desert Survival Training Centre. The instructor wears a 'Daguet' desert camouflage short-sleeve shirt. He is armed with a FAMAS F1 rifle. US Department of Defense

ABOVE: The woodland-type camouflage uniform approved for issue to all French forces in 1991. The pattern is officially called 'Central European' camouflage but is also known as the F2 (correctly a uniform designation) or M91. This camo, copies or developments of the pattern have also been used by Austria, Angola, China, Djibouti, Ethiopia, Gabon, Morocco, Nigeria, and the United Arab Emirates. The F2 uniform differs from the F1 in having no lower pockets although some mis-designations do appear on French manufacturers' labels. Examples of this are 'Daguet' desert uniforms cut to the F1 style but marked 'F2'. This item was made by Seyntex in 2000.

ABOVE: A French soldier training in Germany, 2008. He wears 'Central European' camouflage and is armed with the FAMAS F1. His F2 'Spectra' helmet is fitted with a hit simulator device. US Department of Defense

During Bright Star 01-02, a multinational exercise held in Egypt, a French sniper (right) explains the capabilities of the FR F2 rifle to a Greek soldier. Both wear their respective desert camouflage uniforms, the Greek soldier sporting a US-issue 'Choc-Chip' boonie hat. US Department of Defense

French Brigadier General Oberto, Commander of the SFOR Multinational Brigade, inspects members of the Brigade, Mostar, Bosnia and Herzegovina, 2003. The General wears the 'Central European' camouflage F2 uniform (with French tri-colour sleeve flags). In the background are two members of the Spanish Guardia Civil. US Department of Defense

Germany

ABOVE: SS spot camouflage used by an MG34 team. This was one of a number of camouflage pattern used by SS units during the Second World War and the basis of a number of post-war designs.

LEFT: 'Splittertarnmuster 31' (or 'Splittermuster 31') fabric was developed for use on the Zeltbahn 31 (tent section 1931). The camouflage scheme later formed the base for a number of garments used by the Heer and Luftwaffe (Air Force) during the Second World War. This Luftwaffe *tarnjacke* (camouflage field jacket) uses the Splittertarnmuster 31 camouflage. Garment courtesy Bob Stedman

The Luftwaffe 'Splittertarnmuster 31' *tarnjacke* in use by an airman attached to ground units serving in Russia.

Bundeswehr ('BW', German Armed Forces) 'Splittermuster' (splinter pattern) camouflage jacket issued to the newly formed Federal German armed forces from 1956. The provision of this garment was short-lived and manufacture was discontinued around 1959 when the BW moved to a plain olive green uniform in line with the USA and other Western European armies. It remained in limited use for a time after and the scheme was retained for use as helmet covers well into the 1970s. The camouflage scheme was undoubtedly based on the pre war 'Splittertarnmuster 31'. This jacket was made in 1957.

LEFT: Bundesgrenzschutz (BGS) 'Sumpfmuster' (marsh pattern) camouflage. This pattern was used by German border guards during the Cold War and was based on a pattern used during the Second World War. This camouflage was also used by Libya.

ABOVE: 'Flecktarn' camouflage was authorized for issue to the Bundeswehr in the late 1970s, following a series of trials. However, it was not until 1990 that issue of a 'Flecktarn' combat uniform was actually undertaken in quantity. The name is derived from the German words *fleck* ('spot') and *tarn* ('camouflage'). It was one of a number of designs that had been originally trialled in 1976. 'Flecktarn' camouflage, copies or developments based upon the pattern have also been used by Belgium, Brazil, China, Denmark, Georgia, Japan, Poland and Ukraine.

SFOR troops from the 2nd Reinforced Infantry Company undertaking an insurgent search exercise, Pazaric, Bosnia and Herzegovina, 2002. The men wear standard 'Flecktarn' camouflage uniforms, with matching helmet covers, body armour and load-bearing equipment.

The German national sleeve flag, worn on both sleeves of most camouflage clothing. This shirt also bears the 'GERMANY' titles used by some units deployed outside of Germany.

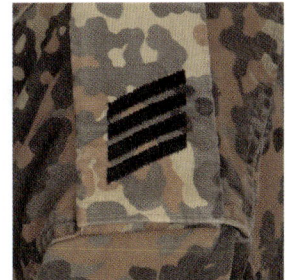

Bundeswehr Rangschlaufen (rank slide) for a Stabsgefreiter (Staff Corporal). Rank designations are worn on both shoulders of camouflage uniforms.

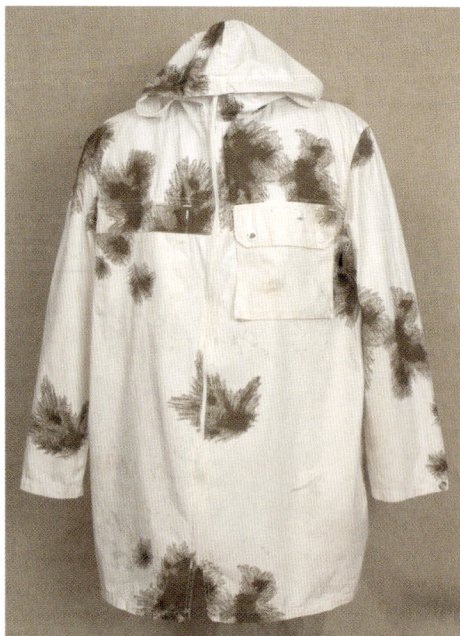

LEFT: 'Schneetarn' (snow camouflage) over-smock. This hooded reversible garment is worn over normal clothing. One side has this mix of white and green 'fir-tree' camouflage for use in woodland, the other is plain white for use in open areas of snow. In either orientation the breast pocket is on the left side. Earlier patterns were of a heavier fabric and used a button fastening rather than the zipper fitted to this example.

RIGHT: 'Wüstentarn' (desert camouflage) was adopted for desert use in 1989 with widespread issue from 1993. Based on the 'Flecktarn' scheme, it is also incorrectly known as 'Troppentarn'. This is the 'Wüstentarn' desert parka, a copy of the standard 'Flecktarn' parka.

LEFT: A Bundeswehr Fähnrich (Officer Cadet) photographed during multinational exercises in Egypt during 2001. He wears a 'Wüstentarn' shirt, with matching bush hat. He is pictured with a Greek soldier, identified by his 'HELLAS' sleeve emblem, wearing a two-tone desert camouflage. US Department of Defense

RIGHT: An armoured vehicle crewman mans an MG3 (a 7.62mm version of the Second World War 7.92mm MG42) during deployment with ISAF in Afghanistan. He wears 'Wüstentarn' uniform with 'Flecktarn' body armour (current body armour is now also produced in 'Wüstentarn'). ISAF

LEFT: During 1995 the Bundeswehr trialled new camouflage uniforms in an effort to find a new temperate scheme that was similar to other NATO forces, which typically used a woodland or DPM scheme. This item, styled on the standard Bundeswehr shirt, was one of the patterns used in the trials. It has a brown-dominant woodland camouflage.

RIGHT: A variant of the pattern used in the 1995 trials for camouflage schemes. This pattern is green-dominant woodland.

Great Britain

RIGHT: *Smocks, Denison, Airborne Troops* (also found labelled as *Smock, Denison, Airborne Troops*). This was the first camouflage garment issued to British forces, being provided for men of the fledgling airborne forces in 1941 to a design developed by Major Denison.

The camouflage uses distinct broad swathes of green over red/brown on a tan base, appearing as if it had been applied using a large paste brush. The intermittent ragged edges gave rise to the name 'Brushstrokes'.

LEFT: The *Smock, Denison, Airborne Troops* in use by a paratrooper in Normandy, June 1944. Although synonymous with airborne troops, the Denison was used by snipers, Commandos and other units.

BELOW: *Smock, Windproof, Camouflaged.* This camouflage uses broad, ragged-edge brushstrokes, similar to those used on the Denison, with green, and two shades of red/brown on a light brick red, almost pink, base. Often cited as being for issue to special forces and the SAS, it was actually a standard issue and was provided to many units of the 21st Army Group during the harsh winter of 1944/45, including members of the ATS. This example is dated 1944 and is of a pullover design. Post-war issues used a full-length zip and continued in production at least until the 1960s. The smock became a badge of office among Royal Marines mountain leaders and was still to be seen in use with members of the *cadre* well into the 1990s.

RIGHT: The *Oversuit, Tank Crews, Camouflaged* used a camouflage based upon that of the windproof smock. Designed toward the end of the war, the Camouflaged 'Pixie Suit' was only issued in limited quantities.

ABOVE: The windproof smock in use with British troops preparing to undertake an unopposed river crossing in NW Europe 1945.

LEFT: Camouflage jungle shirt produced in 1944 for limited trials. It was found that camouflage was good for static troops but a plain green shirt provided better general camouflage in jungle environments. This was confirmed by American experience in the Pacific during the Second World War and again in SE Asia during the Vietnam conflict. Photo courtesy John Bodsworth

ABOVE RIGHT: *Smock, Denison, Airborne Troops*, 1959 pattern. This was a post-war improvement of the original Denison. It had a full-length zip, woollen cuffs, and a closer cut compared to the previously voluminous Second World War pattern. The camouflage pattern is markedly different from the original design. The smock was replaced by a new DPM (disruptive pattern material) version in 1977 but it remained in use for many years after the introduction of DPM, particularly with senior officers. HRH Prince Charles wore a 1959 pattern smock during 2008 when reviewing a parade of men from the Parachute Regiment following their return from Afghanistan.

The East German 'Flächentarn' was the earliest camouflage pattern provided on general issue as a camouflage over-garment. However, the first nation to equip their entire army with a true camouflage uniform, having more than a single base colour, was Great Britain; adopting the DPM (disruptive pattern material) in 1966, with production of new uniforms beginning in 1968. Widespread issue of the DPM combat uniforms began in 1970.

LEFT: *Jacket, Combat (Tropical)*. This shirt, manufactured in 1978 to a 1976 pattern, has quite distinctive light hues to the DPM camouflage pattern. A lightweight and mosquito-proof garment, it was designed for use in all tropical environments and was also used in hot arid areas prior to the development of a dedicated desert camouflage. DPM was introduced in 1966 as standard all arms.

LEFT: Early 1990s production *Jacket, Combat (Tropical)*, showing the noticeably richer hues of the camouflage pattern of the later-issue garment. Both the 1970s and 1990s shirts were manufactured to the same NATO specification number 8415-99-132-3804, but differ noticeably in colour.

RIGHT: Comparison of the richer hues of the DPM fabric used in the late-production tropical jacket (left) with the 1978 production (right).

ABOVE: DPM *Smock, Combat, Windproof, Arctic.* This smock was issued to the author while serving with 3 Commando Brigade RM. As with other specialist garments such as sniper and para smocks, these are not on general issue but are prized by those who are provided with them – or can scrounge one.

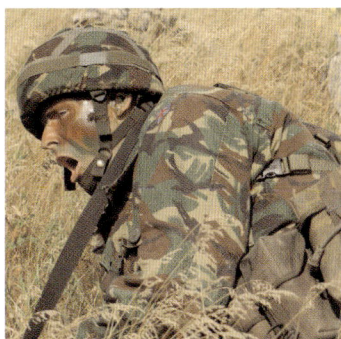

ABOVE: A Scots Guard photographed during Exercise *Patriot 2006*, wearing the DPM Soldier 95 uniform. DPM has undergone a degree of minor change since its introduction and many collectors acknowledge 1966, 1968, 1984, 1990 and 1994 variants. DPM camouflage, copies or developments based upon the pattern have also been used by Angola, Bahrain, Brunei, Cambodia, Canada, Central African Republic, East Timor, Eire, Gambia, Greece, Guinea-Bissau, Indonesia, Iraq, Jordan, Kenya, Kuwait, Malaysia, Nepal, Netherlands, New Zealand, Oman, Pakistan, Philippines, Portugal, Romania, Saudi Arabia, Senegal, Serbia, Sierra Leone, Singapore, Slovenia, Sri Lanka, Sudan, Swaziland, Tanzania and Yemen.

ABOVE RIGHT: A Staff Sergeant of the Staffordshire Regiment serving in Basra, Iraq, during 2005. He wears the standard desert camouflage DDPM CS95 uniform with temperate DPM load-carrying equipment. Author photo

RIGHT: *Jacket, Combat, Lightweight, Desert DPM* two-tone desert shirt issued to the author while serving in Iraq during 1991. The original design of British desert uniform used a three-colour camouflage of tan, brown and black. The pattern was sold to a number of foreign armies, including Iraq's, which then precluded its use by British troops. The two-tone scheme is often referred to as the 'M91 desert' camo.

ABOVE: A pre-production user trials pattern *Jacket, DPM, Combat, Lightweight,* used for field evaluation of the 'Combat Soldier 95' (CS95) uniform. This jacket is similar to the old tropical combat jacket but is void of the left sleeve pen holder and has an added rank tab at the front breast instead of shoulder epaulettes. The approved production-pattern CS95 jacket differed in detail, including the use of Canadian pattern buttons using fabric loop attachment.

RIGHT: At the time of writing, temperate DPM and the two-colour desert variant DDPM are the UK standard camouflage, although research into camouflage uniforms is ongoing. A four-colour desert camouflage has been produced and trialled on field uniforms and Osprey body armour. This rank slide for a Corporal has been produced using the four-colour desert camouflage. It retains the original DDPM tan and brown but has two additional colours: off-white and drab green.

Greece

ABOVE: Greek 'Lizard' camouflage worn by an infantryman armed with an anti-tank launcher. The soldier's load-bearing equipment is also made up in 'Lizard' camouflage. HQNATO

ABOVE: Greek 'Lizard' pattern camouflage jacket. It uses the typical 'Lizard' scheme of a tan base overprinted with green and brown brushstrokes. Greek paratrooper wings are worn on the left breast pocket. Photo courtesy Sean McElwain

LEFT: Fähnrich Jens Kempf of the Bundeswehr instructs Greek soldiers in the operating principles of the MG3 machine gun, prior to a practice firing, during a joint forces small-arms training course held at Mubarak Military City, Egypt 2002. The soldiers wear two-tone brown on tan desert camouflage with green 'Lizard' LBE. US Department of Defense

Hungary

RIGHT: Hungarian M90 pattern camouflage shirt. The uniforms issued as a part of the M90 clothing system all used the same camouflage, termed 'M90' by collectors. The collar points bear the rank badges of a Fotörzsormester (Master Sergeant). The shirt has 'sawn-off' sleeves, a common practice for use during summer months or in warm climates. This item is dated 2002.

LEFT: Hungarian tri-colour national flag patch worn on the left shoulder of all camouflage uniforms.

LEFT: The 'IFOR' (Intervention FORce – NATO and multinational force in Bosnia Herzegovina) patch worn on the right shoulder. It also shows 'IFOR' in Cyrillic script.

ABOVE: This Hungarian anti-aircraft missile operator wears a jacket using the M90 camouflage. His helmet, an Israeli 'Orlite' export, has a cover of the same camouflage, with an added net and scrim. Hungarian Army

RIGHT: A Hungarian RPG team wear white snow camouflage suits over their standard winter uniforms. Hungarian Army

India

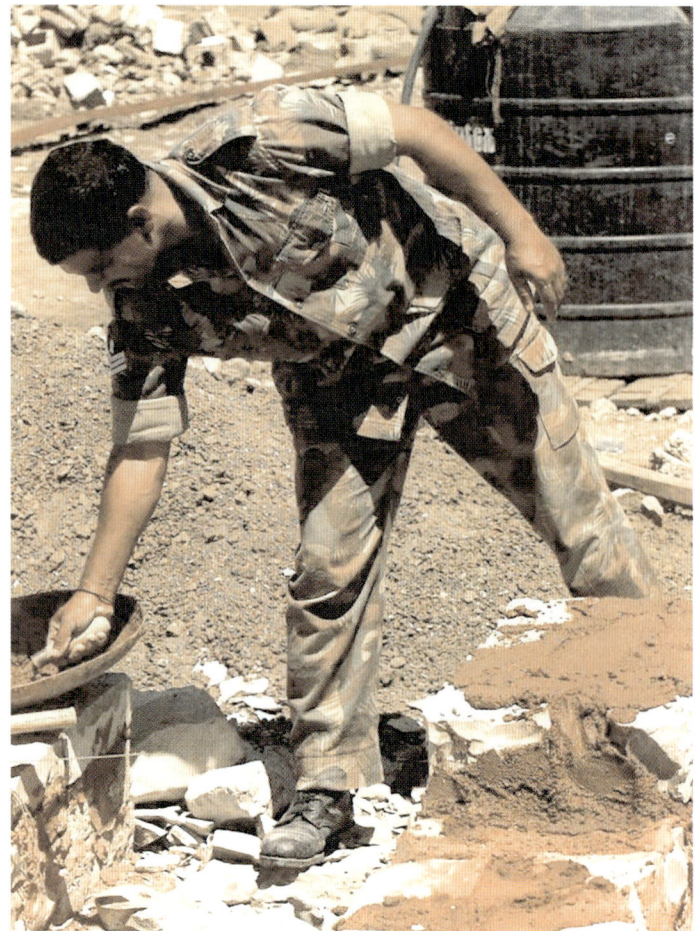

LEFT: Indian camouflage bush jacket dating to the 1980s. This heavyweight garment uses the unique dark and light brown and green on tan base 'Fern' or 'Bush' pattern camouflage.

ABOVE: An Indian Army Company Quartermaster Havildar (Staff Sergeant) laying stones as part of the construction of a well in Somalia as a part of relief efforts under Operation *Restore Hope*. He wears the 'Fern' pattern camouflage uniform. US Department of Defense

LEFT: Indian soldiers of the 9th Battalion Sikh Infantry undertake small-arms training. They wear the current Indian camouflage uniform that uses a somewhat large print woodland-type camouflage. US Department of Defense

ABOVE: The Indian 08 pattern digital camouflage developed by HyperStealth and licensed for production to HyperStealth India. Image courtesy Guy Cramer/HyperStealth

Indonesia

RIGHT: Indonesian police camouflage jacket. This jacket uses an interesting dark brown and green vertical camouflage with blue/grey and yellow highlights. The jacket is fully reversible to plain green.

LEFT: Reverse of the Indonesian police jacket, showing the alternative plain green interior with double-sided zip, four pockets and waist drawstring. The collar holds a concealed lightweight hood.

LEFT: Indonesian police and Marines photographed during public-order training. DPM and US woodland camouflage patterns are evident. US Department of Defense

BELOW: Indonesian paratroopers from a combat control team prepare to jump from a C-130 aircraft during a 1990 exercise. They wear DPM pattern camouflage uniforms. US Department of Defense

Iraq

RIGHT: Iraqi camouflage shirt, one of several camouflage schemes in use with Iraqi forces during the first Gulf War. It is believed that this shirt was made in Romania and uses a typically Romanian style of camouflage with black 'twigs' on a brown, green and tan base. Badged to the infamous Republican Guard, this particular item was recovered by the author while serving in Iraq during 1991.

RIGHT: Iraqi Tactical Support Unit Ra´Id (Major), photographed in Basra in 2005. He wears an urban camouflage uniform with a base colour of sky blue overprinted with medium blue and black. Author photo

ABOVE: Similar to the camouflage shirt above, this example uses the same camouflage scheme but with a brown, green and lime green base instead of the brown, green and tan. It is otherwise identical in style.

The red triangle badge of the Iraqi Republican Guard. It was worn on both sleeves of camouflage and utility uniforms.

The label found in the neck of Iraqi shirts and jackets. It shows the size and maker and bears the triangular Iraqi Government property mark (the equivalent of the British 'broad arrow') and is found on most Iraqi army equipment.

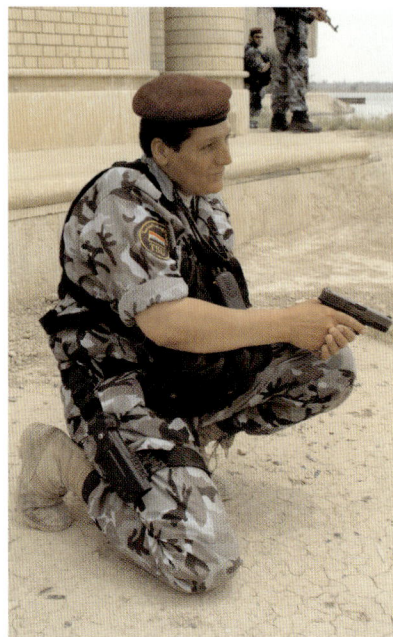

LEFT: A variant of the urban camouflage worn by a member of the Iraqi police TSU. This design shows a four-colour scheme. A similar pattern has also been produced using a digital camouflage. Author photo

ABOVE: Iraqi National Police QRF (Quick Reaction Force) officers parade during a graduation ceremony. The men wear the Iraqi police digital pattern urban camouflage uniform. US Department of Defense

ABOVE: Tan-base camouflage shirt overprinted with widely dispersed green, brown and black. This garment has been identified as Iraqi but is less common than the Romanian-style camouflage.

RIGHT: An Iraqi soldier wearing the standard US six-colour 'Choc-Chip' DBDU desert camouflage uniform observes passing US troops during Operation *Iraqi Freedom*. US Department of Defense

An Iraqi female soldier undergoing weapons training at the Jordanian Royal Military Academy. She wears a jacket with camouflage based on the US woodland scheme. US Department of Defense

Soldiers of 6th Battalion Iraqi Special Operations Force conduct a casualty assessment during an exercise held in Basra 2008. They wear a unique camouflage scheme using dark tan, red/brown, and light green over a tan base. US Department of Defense

ABOVE: The original of this camouflage pattern was introduced in 1929 for shelter halves. From 1937 a modified, less repetitive, version was used for camouflage uniforms issued to Italian paratroopers. This basic pattern was used by the Italian Army for almost seventy years but was superseded by a woodland pattern. White Savoy stars are placed on each collar point of the jacket.

ABOVE: After the Second World War, the San Marco battalion (Italian Marines, a regiment rather than battalion since the mid-1990s) was disbanded, but re-formed in 1965. At this time the unit adopted its own type of camouflage using three colours, similar to the M29, but of a different pattern design. The collar stars are green on Marine uniforms.

LEFT: In the early 1990s the Italian forces reviewed the old camouflage design and both the Marines and Army adopted new patterns. In 1992, the Battaglione San Marco introduced a distinct five-colour pattern using small sections of colour with soft edges. The interesting mix of colours consisted of light tan, green, brown, stone grey and black. The winged lion insignia of the San Marco Marines is fixed to the left breast-pocket flap. The jacket is dated 1997.

ABOVE: An Italian Marine, armed with a Beretta SC70/90 rifle, provides cover for a boarding team approaching a dhow in the North Arabian Sea, 2004. He wears the distinctive San Marco camouflage. US Department of Defense

LEFT: The insignia of the Battaglione San Marco is St Mark's lion, from the coat of arms of Venice. This honour was gained following the defence of Venice during the Austrian offensive of 1918.

ABOVE: Italian Army M92 woodland pattern *uniforme da combattimento e servizio* ('combat and service uniform'), using a four-colour camouflage scheme. The Italian *tricolore* shield is fitted to the left shoulder, with a rank patch for a Corporal attached centrally at the breast. This shirt was made in 1999.

LEFT: Detail of the Italian *tricolore* flag device worn on the left shoulder of camouflage uniforms.

ABOVE: Using a pattern similar to that used on the M92 woodland camouflage, the Italian desert uniform uses a camouflage composed of light tan, medium tan, green and reddish brown.

RIGHT: An Italian Army *bersaglieri* (light infantry) soldier, wearing the unit's distinctive fez, blows a trumpet call while an Honour Guard stands to attention. Tallil Air Base, Iraq, 2004. US Department of Defense

LEFT: The current Italian Army camouflage is the 'Vegetata'. At a casual glance it appears to be a digital camouflage, but on closer examination the camouflage scheme is not pixelated. This rip-stop fabric shirt was made by ATI. INDUYCO in 2005. The tape on the right breast reads 'ESERCITO' (Italian for 'army').

ABOVE: Italian soldiers check a weapons find in the Musahi Valley area, south of Kabul. The men all wear the 'Vegetata' camouflage uniform. Courtesy ISAF

Jamaica

RIGHT: Jamaican Defence Force lightweight jungle fatigue shirt. The camouflage is a typical woodland pattern. Jamaica is one of many nations who have made the wearing of camouflage illegal for anyone who is not a serving member of the military forces.

LEFT: A Jamaican special operations soldier runs fully armed during Exercise *Fuerzas Commando 07*, held in Honduras. He wears a woodland camouflage uniform.

Japan

RIGHT: Japanese 1980 pattern camouflage shirt. It uses brown, red/brown and green over a tan/grey base.

LEFT: A Japanese Self Defence Force soldier wearing the M80 camouflage uniform during joint US/Japanese Exercise *Orient Shield '85*. US Department of Defense

BELOW: JSDF 1995 pattern camouflage uniform, which replaced the M80 pattern. Photo courtesy Sean McElwain

RIGHT: Manufacturer's label on Japanese shirt, showing it was produced in 1983.

BELOW: The Japanese pattern 1995 uniform is a 'Flecktarn'-type print using brown, light green and black flecks on a tan base. These JSDF soldiers were photographed during 2008. US Department of Defense

Jordan

ABOVE: KA2 digital desert camouflage uniform. HyperStealth Biotechnology Corp developed the KA2 (King Abdullah II) series for the Jordanian forces. Seven different camouflage patterns are currently in use with the Jordanian Army, Air Force, Navy, Special Forces, Royal Guard, Public Security (Police Force), Civil Defense and Customs. Photo courtesy Sean McElwain

RIGHT: HRH Prince Ali wearing the KA2 Royal Guard digital camouflage uniform provided only to members of the Royal Family and the elite Jordanian Royal Guard. Image courtesy Guy Cramer/HyperStealth

BELOW: US Air Force Col. Gregory Graf, left, talks with His Royal Highness Prince Feisal Bin Al Hussein, Special Assistant to Chairman of the Joint Chiefs of Staff of Jordanian Armed Forces. The prince wears the Jordanian KA2 digital desert camouflage uniform introduced in 2003. US Department of Defense

The Jordanian Army's current-issue KA2 digital woodland camouflage uniform. Photo courtesy Sean McElwain

KA2 'Public Security Directorate urban digital' camouflage uniform as used by the Jordanian Police. It is similar to the blue/grey uniform worn by the Civil Defence Directorate. Photo courtesy Sean McElwain

The Jordanian 'Rocks' pattern waterproof camouflage parka. The design is reversible from 'rocks' to a design based on the camouflage used on the US desert night parka. Photo courtesy Sean McElwain

Korea
(Republic of)

ABOVE: 'Duck Hunter' camouflage jacket used by Republic of Korea Marine Corps during the 1960s. This camouflage scheme saw use in Vietnam with RKMC units. The camouflage is based on the Second World War American 'Frog Skin' scheme made famous by the USMC during the Pacific campaign. The term 'Duck Hunter' was only coined during the post-Second World War period when this pattern was reproduced in quantity for the American civilian hunters' market, but it is in common useage with collectors. The left breast pocket of this shirt has an ink-stamped 'RKMC' logo.

ABOVE: A 1970s Korean Army 'Noodle' camouflage jacket badged to a Sang-Byong (corporal) of the paratroops. It uses brown, black and green on a light green base to produce the camouflage scheme. In addition to the three-bar corporal rank device, it bears parachute unit insignia as well as basic paratrooper and parachute rigger wings above the left breast pocket.

LEFT: Airborne wings worn on the left breast of the 'Noodle' camouflage jacket. Above is the Korean army basic parachute wing; worn below is the parachute rigger qualification wing.

LEFT: Korean Army paratroops' patch worn on the left shoulder of the 'Noodle' camouflage jacket.

ABOVE RIGHT: 1970 Republic of Korea Marine Corps camouflage shirt. It uses four colours in a unique large and bold pattern. It bears the insignia of the Marine's Amphibious Recon unit and parachute wings. The field camouflage uniform is less ornate in its use of insignia and has an ink-stamped 'RKMC' logo on the left pocket rather than the embroidered pattern shown here. This camouflage was also used by Chilean forces.

RIGHT: Pocket insignia fitted on the right breast of the Korean Marines shirt. It is the patch of the RKMC Amphibious Reconnaissance unit.

RIGHT: Korean desert camouflage jacket, which uses a camouflage inspired by the American DBDU's 'Choc-Chip' scheme, but with a greater concentration of the black and white chips. This camouflage was used by Korean units serving in Iraq and Afghanistan.

ABOVE: Republic of Korean Navy camouflage shirt using a highly repetitive woodland-type camouflage. It bears the insignia of a combat diver specialist.

LEFT: Detail of Korean Navy diver insignia worn above the left breast pocket.

LEFT: Republic of Korean Navy diver insignia worn on the left shoulder.

ABOVE: Korea national flag sleeve insignia worn on the left sleeve of the desert uniform (and all camouflage uniforms when serving outside of Korean national territory).

ABOVE: Second-pattern Korean desert camouflage uniform as worn in Iraq and Afghanistan and other arid regions. It is badged to a Byong-Yang (sergeant).

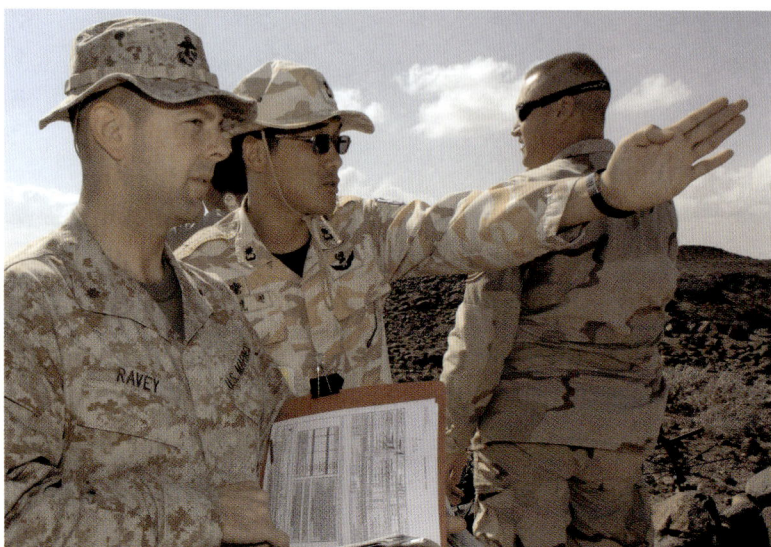

LEFT: Djibouti, 2007. At left a US Marine Corps Major, wearing Desert MARPAT Camouflage, discusses a close air support mission with a South Korean So-Ryong (Major) wearing desert camouflage. At right, a US soldier wears the DCU camouflage.

ABOVE: Korea 2007. A RKMC Sang-Byong (Corporal) Military Policeman. He wears the woodland camouflage uniform with colourful gold and red RKMC MP embellishments. US Department of Defense

ABOVE: Current RKMC woodland camouflage winter coat. Similar camouflage pattern to the Navy shirt but in a noticeably more vivid print. Garment courtesy Eastwestrading

RIGHT: RKMC rank insignia for a Chung-Wi (1st Lieutenant), as worn on the winter coat. Garment courtesy Eastwestrading

ABOVE: 1980s jacket using a variant of the woodland camouflage. It is badged to a Ha Sa (Staff Sergeant) of paratroops. The Korean master paratrooper wings are worn on the left breast with US army master paratrooper wings on the right breast.

LEFT: Korean Marines on field exercise wearing woodland pattern camouflage uniforms.

Kuwait

Coat, Desert Camouflage Pattern: Combat. This later-production American tri-colour DCU garment has a pen pocket on the right sleeve and epaulette straps at the shoulders. Made to a standard US military contract, it was supplied to the Kuwait Army under the military assistance programme. It has a 'KUWAIT ARMY' tape on the left breast and the name 'Ali N. Bourisli' on the right breast.

Kuwait digital desert camouflage uniform. These uniforms were imported from China c. 2006. Photo courtesy Sean McElwain

BELOW: During 2002 Kuwaiti Commandos from Unit 25 parade in desert camouflage uniforms. The Kuwaiti desert camouflage worn here is a simple dark brown on light yellow base. The difference between the cap and tunic indicates how the colouring weathers.

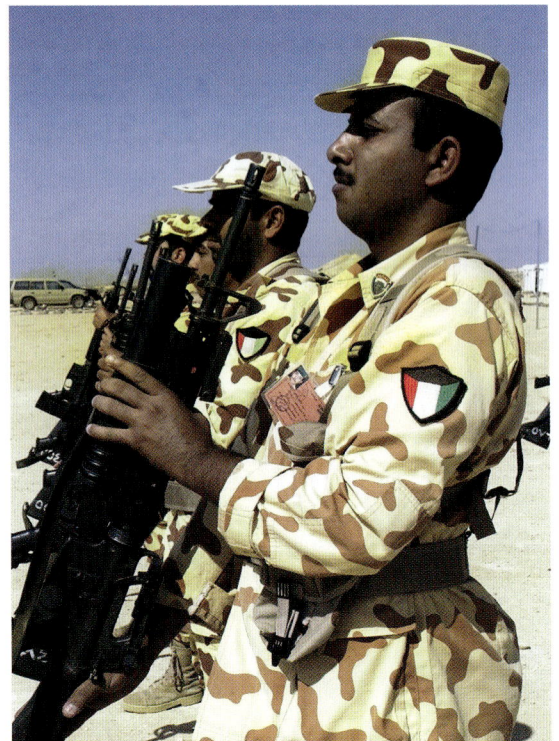

Lithuania

Lithuanian field uniform, made up of fabric printed with a camouflage copied directly from the US M81 woodland scheme. It has a frontal rank flap badged to a Vyresnysis Leiutenant (First Lieutenant).

ABOVE: The Lithuanian national flag insignia worn on the pocket flap on the upper left sleeve.

LEFT: Lithuanian troops wearing woodland camouflage field uniforms and load-bearing equipment. The camouflage is US M81 woodland.

Malaysia

RIGHT: Malaysian camouflage uniform of the 1970s. It has a green and brown 'Brushstroke' camouflage on a tan base. The base fabric is an aertex-type fabric similar to that used on British tropical clothing of Second World War vintage.

BELOW: Current Malaysian woodland pattern jungle uniform. It uses a woodland pattern camouflage printed in a distinct horizontal pattern, giving rise to the name 'Woodland Tigerstripe'. Garment courtesy Eastwestrading

ABOVE: Mejar (Major) Lee photographed wearing the Malaysian 'Woodland Tigerstripe'-type camouflage uniform during a jungle training exercise held in 2002. US Department of Defense

Netherlands

RIGHT: The Dutch Army uses a close copy of British DPM fabric for temperate combat uniforms. This DPM jacket was manufactured in 1990 by H.v.Puijenbroek.

LEFT: The tri-colour Netherlands flag patch worn on the left sleeve of all Dutch camouflage garments.

LEFT: Desert uniforms are made up using a pattern based on the American three-colour DCU camouflage scheme. Cut identically to the temperate DPM jacket, this item was made by Seyntex in 1997.

LEFT: Majoor (Major) Willem Heesbeen of 804 Air Defense Squadron, Koninklijke Luchtmacht (Royal Netherlands Air Force). Photographed at Eindhoven, Netherlands, during 1999, the Major wears a US-issue DCU camouflage uniform and US PASGT helmet with DCU cover.

ABOVE: A Dutch ISAF soldier wearing the desert pattern camouflage uniform during pre-deployment manoeuvres. Germany, May 2008. US Department of Defense

ABOVE: Jungle camouflage jacket introduced in 1992 for use by Dutch troops serving with UNTAC (United Nations Transitional Authority for Cambodia). This jacket was made by WAHLER in 1993.

ABOVE RIGHT: American *Coat, Hot Weather, Woodland Camouflage Pattern; Combat.* This item was introduced for use by the Korps Mariniers in 1993. It is the standard US-manufacture and US-issue coat modified in the Netherlands by the addition of OD rank epaulettes at the shoulders and the 'Korps Mariniers' title. Unlike American troops, who wore the name tape above the right breast pocket, the Korps Mariniers wore the name tape above the left breast pocket. This coat was manufactured in 1996.

RIGHT: 'Korps Mariniers' title and OD fabric epaulette that was added to the original US-issue garment.

RIGHT: Typical Dutch rank slide, this example signifying a Sergeant Wachtmeester (Sergeant). Of note is the distinctive Dutch epaulette pattern with velcro fitting and fabric loop. This style of epaulette is used with all Dutch-manufacture camouflage uniforms but it was not used on the modified US garments issued to the Korps Mariniers, which used a standard style without the fabric loop.

RIGHT: A Marinier der 1e Klasse (Marine 1st Class) of the Dutch Korps Mariniers wears the US *Coat, Hot Weather, Woodland Camouflage Pattern; Combat* during an urban warfare exercise. US Department of Defense

Norway

LEFT: The Norwegian M80 camouflage, designed for use in the coniferous woodlands and low mountain areas of Norway. Its camouflage scheme uses green and dark brown patterns over a lime green base.

RIGHT: A Norwegian soldier armed with an MP5 SMG, wearing the M80 camouflage winter jacket with snow camouflage trousers. A snow camouflage over-jacket and helmet cover were also available for use during the Norwegian winter. Norwegian Army

RIGHT: The distinctive camouflage pattern worn by units of the Luftforsvaret (Royal Norwegian Air Force) during the 1980s and 90s.

ABOVE: The Norwegian flag emblem on the right sleeve of the Luftforsvaret camouflage shirt. It is normally worn on all field uniforms.

LEFT: The summer-weight M98 field jacket is based on the US BDU jacket. It uses the same pattern as the winter jacket but different colours: two tones of green over a light brown base. This garment was made by Pioner in 2000.

RIGHT: The summer-weight jacket in use with a Norwegian soldier during an exercise held in Germany 2008.

Pakistan

RIGHT: Pakistani 1980s 'Brushstroke' camouflage jacket. The front and pocket flaps are all secured using highly reflective chromed snap fasteners. Garment courtesy Eastwestrading

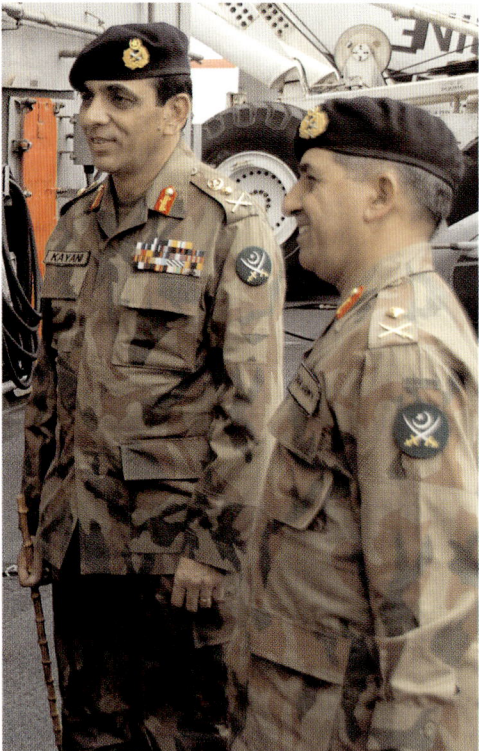

ABOVE: Pakistan Army General Ashfaq Kayani and Major General Ahmad Shuja Pasha, photographed in August 2008. Both wear uniforms using a Pakistani three-colour camouflage of dark green and red brown over dark tan. US Department of Defense

RIGHT: Pakistani troops wearing US M81 woodland-style camouflage uniforms and body armour photographed during a multinational exercise held during 2007. They carry the Belgian FN 2000 rifle. US Department of Defense

Poland

ABOVE: A Wz68 'Moro' pattern winter coat badged to a Pulkownik (Colonel) and dated 1982. The scheme is a light grey over dark grey 'wood-bark' effect. 'Moro' camouflage was introduced in the early 1970s following the adoption of the 'Raindrop' camouflage by East Germany. The East German camouflage was considered too similar to the Polish 'Raindrop' that had been introduced in 1958.

ABOVE RIGHT: Milicja Obywatelska (National Militia) version of the 'Moro' pattern winter coat. It uses a larger print of the camouflage design printed in similar colours to the army version but in greater contrast.

RIGHT: The 'Moro' camouflage was replaced by the Wz89 'Puma' pattern shown here. Typically of many Eastern European camouflage schemes, the pattern is only visible at closer viewing distances; at little more than a few paces, it blends into a single base colour.

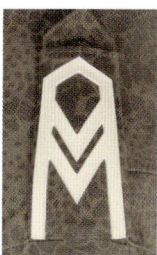

LEFT: Epaulette rank slide in 'Puma' camouflage fabric with white plastic rank marking for a Starszy Sierzant (Staff Sergeant). This winter jacket is dated 1990.

ABOVE: Polish soldiers of the 18th Airborne Assault Battalion tend to a civilian 'casualty' during an urban training exercise held in December 2006 prior to the first Polish deployment to Afghanistan.

LEFT: The Polish four-colour Wz93 'Pantera' (panther) pattern. The Wz93 was a uniform concept on which this camouflage was based. It is a woodland pattern made up of light green, dark green, brown and black. This shirt bears the two silver rank bars of a Kapral (Corporal) on the epaulettes and national flag insignia (not visible). The shirt is marked 'Koszulo-bluza polowa wz. 93' and dated 2006.

ABOVE: Polish national flag insignia worn on both sleeves of the Wz1993 and Wz2000 camouflage uniforms. Also shown are the twin rank bars of a Kapral.

A Polish Army Starszy Szeregowy (Lance Corporal) wearing Wz2000 desert camouflage in Iraq during 2006. Below his national flag insignia he wears the CIMIC (Civil Military Cooperation) title. US Department of Defense

RIGHT: The four-colour Wz2000 'Pantera Pustynna' (desert panther) camouflage scheme introduced for service in Iraq. This shirt was manufactured in 2004.

Portugal

RIGHT: Portuguese 'Lizard' camouflage pattern jacket. This scheme saw use in Portugal's various colonial conflicts and was copied by a number of African armies.

ABOVE: Portuguese model 2000 DPM jacket. Made from a cotton HBT (herringbone twill) fabric, it was manufactured by Dolman Uniforme.

RIGHT: A Portuguese Marine undertaking simulated helicopter inserted boarding operations using the fast roping technique from a Lynx helicopter. He wears a 'Lizard' camouflage jacket. NATO Exercise *Strong Resolve*, 1998. US Department of Defense

ABOVE: Detail of the 'PORTUGAL' title and national colours worn on the left sleeve. The red and green national colours are sometimes replaced by the national flag insignia.

RIGHT: British Lieutenant General Michael Walker, Commander of the Allied Command Europe Rapid Reaction Corps, meets Portuguese soldiers during Operation *Joint Endeavour*, Bosnia, May 1996. The image shows the contrast between the General's British DPM and the Portuguese version of DPM. Portuguese DPM gradually replaced the older 'Lizard' pattern camouflage in the mid 1990s. The troops show a variety of national patches worn on the left sleeve, including the green/red patch and the national flag device. US Department of Defense

Romania

ABOVE: M90 camouflage uniforms worn by Romanian troops undergoing training in the USA during Exercise *Cooperative Osprey 1998*. The camouflage print has a distinctly green dominance when compared to the photograph of the brown-dominant winter coat shown at right. US Department of Defense

LEFT: M93 'Fleck' camouflage uniforms in use during exercise *Cooperative Osprey 1996*. US Department of Defense

ABOVE: M90 woodland camouflage pattern winter coat. The M90 camouflage is also called 'Romanian Leaf' pattern.

LEFT: M02 desert DPM camouflage uniforms in use with Romanian troops serving in Basra, Iraq, during 2005. The radio held by the soldier at left has a cover of M02 temperate DPM fabric. Both camouflage types were based on British DPM. Author photo

Russia

RIGHT: Russian KLMK *Kamuflirovannyi Letnyi Maskirovochnyi Kombinezon* (camouflage summer overall, or M69) reversible coverall showing the two camouflage schemes printed on to this one-piece garment. At left is the green-dominant obverse and at right the reverse. There are camouflage loops fitted at the shoulders, chest and sleeves as well as on the hood.

LEFT: The KLMK one-piece uniform was issued with a matching reversible camouflage mask. Shown here is the reverse side.

The lightweight hessian fabric KZS (*Kostium Zashchitnoi Seti*, or camouflage uniform set). This simple hooded garment was to be worn on its own or over other clothing to provide camouflage. Issued with matching trousers, it was manufactured in a wide variety of shades because of somewhat lax production controls.

Russian VSR woodland (or VSR 93) camouflage. (VSR stands for *Vooruzhennye Sili Rossii*, or Russian Armed Forces.)

ABOVE: Camouflage summer shirt using 'Flora' (VSR 98) camouflage, showing how the camouflage weathers down with use.

RIGHT: Russian airborne troops parade at Tuzla Air Base, Bosnia-Herzegovina. They wear what appear to be a variant of, or well-faded VSR 93 camouflage uniforms. US Department of Defense

ABOVE: Camouflage winter jacket using the 'Flora' (VSR 98) camouflage.

LEFT: Russian Federation sleeve patch bearing the national flag and the legend 'Vooruzhennye Sili Rossii'.

US Army Lieutenant General William E. Ward, Commander, Stabilization Force (COMSFOR), Bosnia and Herzegovina, is briefed by Russian troops. Two Russians wear 'Flora' (VSR 98) Camouflage, while the officer at left wears a VSR woodland camouflage jacket. US Department of Defense

A Russian camouflage jacket bearing a label that shows it was made in Moscow, and designating it as '*spetsodezhda*', or 'special purpose'.

Singapore

RIGHT: Singapore Armed Forces woodland pattern *Shirt, Mans, No.4 Dress, Camouflage*. It is named to 'O H KOO' above the right breast pocket. Dated 1994.

ABOVE: Post-1983 sleeve rank for SAF 2nd Sergeant. The rank chevrons are displayed at each shoulder.

A Master Sergeant of the Tentera Singapura (Singapore land forces) wearing the *No.4 Dress* camouflage uniform. He is armed with the 5.56mm SAR 21 rifle. US Navy photo

Slovenia

'Amoeba' M03 woodland camouflage jacket. Photo courtesy Sean McElwain

Slovenian MPs photographed in Sarajevo during 2003. The men wear Slovenian 'Amoeba' M03 camouflage uniforms and body armour.

A Slovenian soldier serving with ISAF in Afghanistan. Although body armour and equipment make little more than his sleeves visible, he can be seen to be wearing US pattern Desert Combat Uniform (DCU). Slovenia has developed its own desert camouflage scheme based on the temperate M03 pattern, but using a tan base with light green, green and brown camouflage print. Courtesy NATO/ISAF

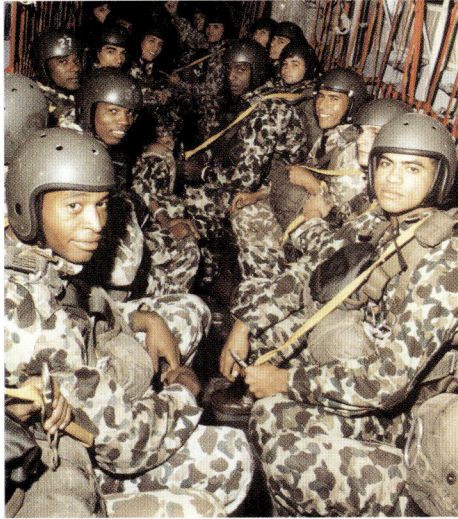

RIGHT: Brazilian Fuzileiros Navais (Naval Rifles, or Marines) camouflage jacket. The camouflage scheme is an interesting variant of the 'Lizard pattern'.

LEFT: 1984. Brazilian paratroopers onboard a C-130 await the order to jump. The men all wear the 'Duck Hunter' pattern camouflage inspired by the US Army's M1942 jungle suit.

LEFT: 'FUZILEIROS NAVAIS' shoulder tab on the Brazilian Marines jacket.

BELOW: Variant of the Brazilian 'Lizard' pattern camouflage. Photo courtesy Sean McElwain

RIGHT: This Salvadorean special forces soldier wears a 'rip-stop' fabric shirt in a woodland camouflage based on the US M81 scheme.

BELOW: Infanteria De Marina (Navy Commandos) of the Chilean Navy. Uniforms and equipment are all woodland camouflage. US Navy photo

LEFT: Colombian 'Duck Hunter'-style camouflage based on the American M42 pattern camouflage. This shirt is badged to a soldier attached to the Multinational Force and Observers (MFO). Colombia provided an infantry battalion to the MFO based in Sinai.

RIGHT: Shoulder insignia of the Multinational Force and Observers (MFO).

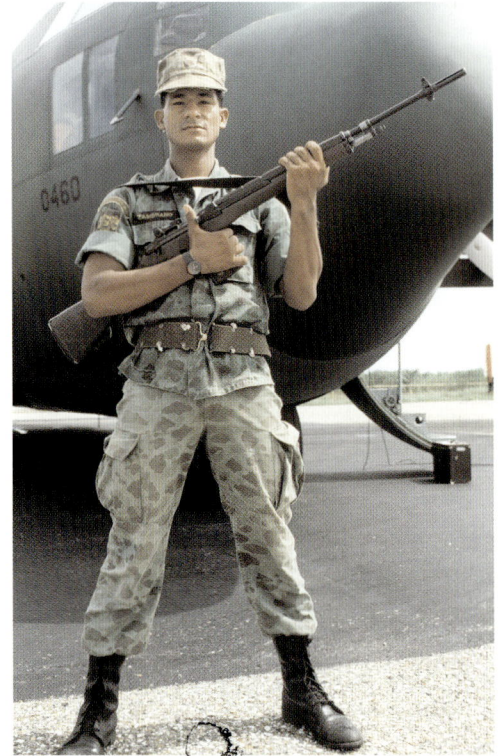

RIGHT: A Colombian marine armed with an M-14 rifle wears a well-used and patched camouflage uniform using the 'Duck Hunter' pattern.

ABOVE: Bolivian army ranks photographed during Exercise *Fuerzas Unidas*. They wear an interesting camouflage using a woodland pattern but with hues better suited to semi-arid terrain.

ABOVE: US Army Major General Alfred A. Valenzuela (centre) explains the details of communications equipment to Bolivian Army Commander-in-Chief, Major General Juan Hurtado Rosales (right). Both men wear the US M81 woodland camouflage jacket. Many countries use US uniforms, direct copies, or variants of the M81 woodland camouflage scheme.

RIGHT: Camouflage shirt worn by commandos and other units of the Ecuadorean armed forces. This garment is badged to the Fuerza Aérea Ecuatoriana (Ecuadorean Air Force). FAE paratrooper wings are worn above the left breast pocket. Photo courtesy Sean McElwain

ABOVE: During exercises held in 1986, Ecuadorean commandos train with an American M72 light anti-tank weapon.

Spain

RIGHT: A Spanish army shirt manufactured in a woodland type camouflage. This garment was produced in 1992.

ABOVE: The national flag device worn on the left sleeve of Spanish camouflage uniforms. Also shown is the rank epaulette showing the two stars of a Teniente Coronel (Lieutenant Colonel).

BELOW: Spanish Air Force forward air controllers set up communications equipment that will allow them to provide close air support for ground troops. They wear Spanish woodland pattern camouflage uniforms. The airman at left wears a US M81 woodland camouflage boonie hat. July 2007. US Department of Defense

Sweden

RIGHT: Swedish M1990 camouflage jacket. The sharp angular shapes of the camouflage pattern are inspired by German Second World War designs.

Swedish national flag insignia worn on the upper left sleeve.

BELOW: The Swedish desert version of the M90 camouflage. It retains the angular pattern but in colours reminiscent of the US DCU uniform. US Department of Defense

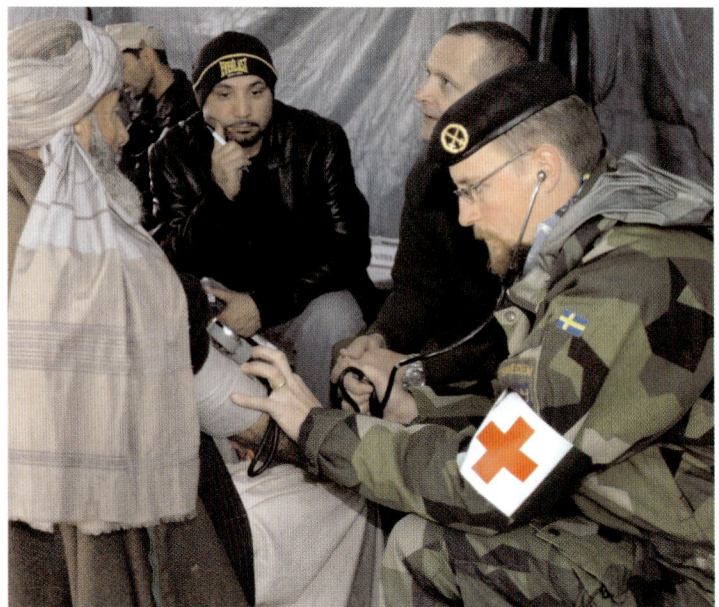

The M90 camouflage *fältjacka* worn by a Swedish military doctor checking Afghan civilians in the Mazar-e Sharif region of Afghanistan, 2006. US Department of Defense

Switzerland

RIGHT: During the early 1950s a reversible double-sided helmet cover with 'Frühlingsfarben' (spring) and 'Herbstfarben' (autumn) camouflage patterns was issued with the blue-grey wool uniform. It was not until the introduction of 'Leibermuster 55' or 'Alpenflage' camouflage that it was applied to combat uniforms. This is a quite distinct and complicated colour scheme, using a stone colour base overprinted with sections of green, red and black, with small white chips overprinted light green. Compared to the now almost universal woodland scheme, it appears quite bright and colourful. This camouflage pattern was first used on the TASS/TAZ 57 field uniform (the name derived from the French *Tenue d'ASSault* and German *TArnanZug*), and was in use between 1957 and 1992.

RIGHT: Swiss army national sleeve device: 'Switzerland' over the Swiss flag.

ABOVE: TASS/TAZ 90 woodland pattern camouflage shirt. This scheme has undoubtedly evolved from the original 'Leibermuster 55', retaining a similar pattern but with a base of mid-brown with dark brown, green and black overprint, the distinct white and light green chips of the original pattern having been deleted. Manufactured by Weder Meir.

RIGHT: Swiss soldiers march-past during the opening ceremony for Exercise *Combined Endeavor 2008*, held in Germany. The men all wear the TASS/TAZZ 90 woodland camouflage uniform. US Department of Defense

Thailand

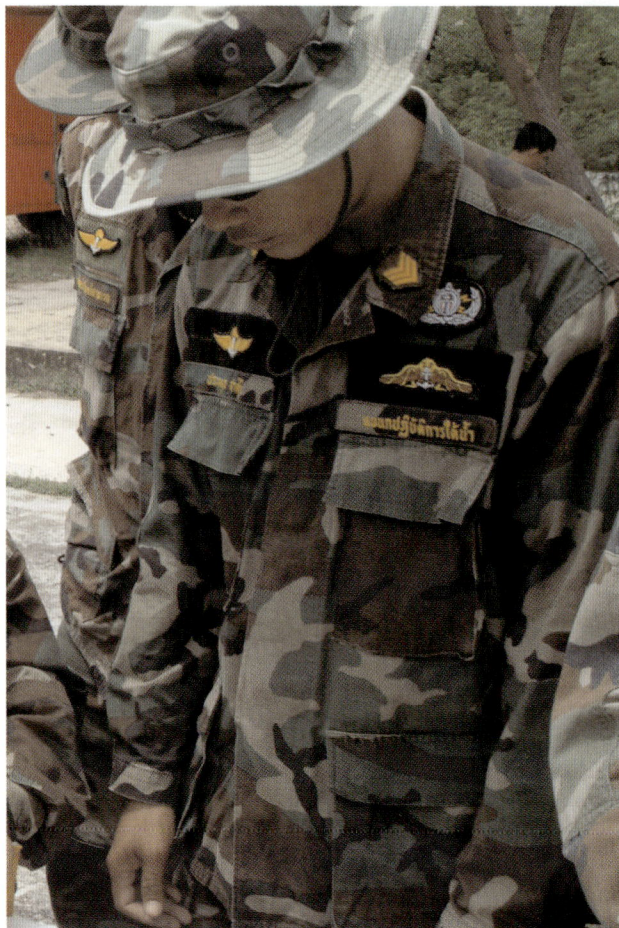

LEFT: A Royal Thai Navy (RTN) issue woodland camouflage jacket. It is badged to a paratrooper EOD specialist Ja Eg (petty officer 1st class).

ABOVE: The RTN woodland camouflage jacket in use. This example is similarly badged to the preceding studio image, including the Ja Eg rank and paratrooper insignia. US Department of Defense

ABOVE: An interesting photo taken using night-vision equipment (NVG). It shows a US Jump Master at left, checking the static lines of Thai paratroopers prior to a jump over Lop Buri, Thailand, May 24, 2006. This is a good example of the appearance of woodland camouflage under IR illumination.

RIGHT: Soldiers of the 3rd battalion 3rd Company Kings Guards on exercise. The lead soldier, a Sip Eg (Sergeant), is wearing a uniform using a camouflage inspired by the green-dominant US ERDL pattern.

Turkey

RIGHT: Turkish woodland camouflage shirt. The camouflage print is noticeably limited in its repetition, with the large tan print patch above the left breast pocket being repeated below that pocket, below the left skirt pocket and again on the right skirt pocket. This shirt was made in Istanbul during 1999.

ABOVE: 'Turkiye' sleeve patch worn on the left shoulder of all camouflage uniforms by Turkish troops.

LEFT: Photographed in 2000, this Onbasi (Private first class) of the Turkish paratroops wears the standard Turkish woodland pattern camouflage uniform with sky-blue beret. The Onbasi's load-bearing equipment uses the same camouflage.

ABOVE: Turkish airmen undergo ground defence training during 2007. The airmen wear woodland load bearing vests over US issue woodland camouflage Interceptor armour. Uniforms are Turkish Air Force 'urban' blue camouflage clothing. US Department of Defense

Ukraine

ABOVE: This Ukrainian camouflage is based on the Russian woodland pattern introduced in the early 1980s. It is often termed 'Little Oak' pattern by collectors.

LEFT: Ukrainian Marines undertake training prior to deployment with IFOR during 1996. The Marines wear 'Little Oak' camouflage uniforms with covers of the same fabric on the Russian STSh 81 'Sphera' helmets.

ABOVE: Germany 2004. The Little Oak' camouflage uniforms worn by these troops use a light green base, replacing the light tan. At the extreme left of the front rank is an example of a well-faded standard example or possibly an autumn variant. US Department of Defense

RIGHT: A Ukrainian Army soldier armed with a PKM LMG stands atop a BRT-80A APC, Al Kut, Iraq. He wears the Ukrainian desert camouflage uniform with a load-bearing vest made up in US tri-colour desert fabric.

USA

ABOVE: Cape Torokina, Bouganville, 1943. A group of war-weary Marine Raiders. All are wearing the USMC first-pattern two-piece camouflage uniform and helmet covers of the same M42 fabric. US National Archive

ABOVE: The US Army one-piece M1942 camouflage uniform. Although the green-dominant side is designed for outerwear (shown at right), it was possible to reverse the garment to wear the tan-dominant camouflage outermost (left). However, the supporting braces were on the inner side (but usually cut off!) and the pockets were on the green side. This camouflage is often called 'Duck Hunter', as it was popularized by American hunters in the post-war years. It was known as 'Frogskin' during the Second World War.

ABOVE: The USMC M42 camouflage jacket showing the green-dominant side (five-colour). It has two internal breast pockets closed by snaps and four front fastening buttons marked 'US MARINE CORPS'.

RIGHT: USMC camouflage jacket showing the tan side (four-colour). The garment was not designed to be worn reversed; it merely used the double-sided fabric originally seen on the Army's one-piece M42 camouflage suit. However, photographic evidence shows that it was on occasion worn with the tan side outermost.

LEFT: Vietnam-period *Coat, Man's, Camouflage Cotton, Wind Resistant Poplin, Class 2*. This rip-stop coat is made up in the green-dominant 'Lowland' ERDL camouflage designed by the Engineer Research and Development Laboratories and also known as the M65 camouflage. The camouflage coat began to replace the plain OD tropical combat jacket during 1967. Early production coats were made of plain cotton poplin.

ABOVE: *Coat, Man's, Camouflage Cotton, Wind Resistant Poplin, Class 2*, first issued in 1968. This garment uses the brown-dominant 'Highland' camouflage generally associated with the USMC but also used by the Army. Despite the different camouflage dominance, there is no distinction in the garment labelling between the green 'Lowland' or brown 'Highland' patterns.

BELOW: The 'Airborne' tab and insignia of the US Army's Civil Affairs and Psychological Command. In Iraq, members of this unit delivered air-drop propaganda and surrender leaflets from Black Hawk helicopters fitted with loudspeakers that would broadcast messages in Arabic as well as the high-decibel strains of *Ride of the Valkyrie*!

ABOVE: *Coat, Combat, Woodland Camouflage Pattern*. The M81 'Woodland' camouflage scheme was an enlarged version of the brown-dominant ERDL scheme. This BDU (Battle Dress Uniform) jacket was used by Sergeant First Class Saur of the Civil Affairs and Psychological Command. On the left sleeve, below an 'Airborne' tab, is the insignia of the Civil Affairs and Psychological Command. Above the left breast pocket are the parachutist badge and basic aviation wings, and on the right breast pocket is the Drill Instructor's badge. The BDU was manufactured in cotton and rip-stop fabrics.

The author obtained this BDU jacket from Sergeant Saur in exchange for a British-issue DPM camouflage NBC (CBRN) protective suit while serving in Iraq in 1991.

ABOVE: Post-Vietnam *Coat, Hot Weather, Camouflage Pattern*. This is often called the 'RDF' (Rapid Deployment Force) camouflage and was on issue to the USMC and select units such as the 82nds and 101st Airborne Divisions from the mid-1970s. It uses similar colours to the Vietnam-period brown-dominant 'Highland' ERDL camouflage and is of a similar cut but has vertical breast pockets and straight pocket flaps.

RIGHT: *Coat, Aircrew, Camouflage Pattern; Combat, Woodland Camouflage Class 1,* a fire-retardant garment made for aircrew, also known as the Aircrew Battle Dress Uniform (ABDU). The fabric is 92% Meta-Aramid, 5% Para-Aramid and 3% static dissipative fibre. The Meta-Aramid (NOMEX) provides good wear and fire-retarding properties while Para-Armid (Kevlar) improves wear. The camouflage is the standard M81 woodland pattern, but this is a good example of how colours can appear different because of the fabric used in the construction. The pattern was also produced in desert camouflage. This particular coat was made in 2000.

ABOVE LEFT: A US Sergeant First Class photographed in Northern Iraq during 1991, wearing the M81 'Woodland' camouflage uniform, helmet cover and body armour. US M81 'Woodland' camouflage, copies or developments based upon the pattern have also been used by Afghanistan, Albania, Argentina, Bolivia, Bosnia, Cambodia, Chile, China, Colombia, Côte d'Ivoire, Croatia, Cyprus, Dominican Republic, Ecuador, Georgia, Greece, Ghana, Guatemala, Honduras, Iran, Iraq, Italy, Jordan, Latvia, Lebanon, Liberia, Lithuania, Luxembourg, Macedonia, Mali, Mexico, Netherlands, Nicaragua, Nigeria, Pakistan, Palestine, Peru, Portugal, Russia, Rwanda, Senegal, Serbia, Sierra Leone, South Korea, Sri Lanka, Syria, Thailand, Uganda, Venezuela, and Yemen. Author photo

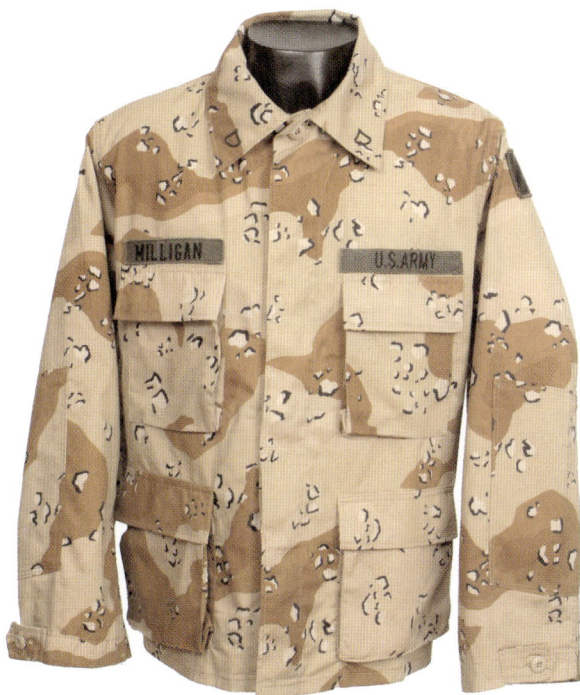

BELOW: Black on OD subdued 3rd Infantry badge worn on the left sleeve of the DBDU uniform.

RIGHT: Gen. Norman Schwarzkopf, Commander-in-Chief, US Central Command, talks with Maj. Gen. Barry McCaffrey, Commanding General, 24th Infantry Division. Both officers are wearing the DBDU uniform used by all US troops during Desert Storm, 1991.

ABOVE: 'Choc-Chip' camouflage Desert Battle Dress Uniform (DBDU), *Coat, Camouflage Pattern: Desert*. This camouflage was first issued in 1983 and was the standard uniform of US forces during Desert Storm (1st Gulf War) in 1990. This 1985-dated garment is badged to the 3rd Infantry Division using ordinary black on OD insignia. This was standard practice on the DBDU. The collar points display the rank badges of a Private First Class (PFC).

RIGHT: The *Parka, Night Camouflage, Desert* was first tested in 1982 and later used operationally during the 1st Gulf War. The camouflage consists of small dark grey squares in a uniform grid design over a dark sage green base with intermittent dark green splotches. The pattern was designed to interfere with image-intensifying sights and to reduce the signature on IR night-vision devices. The scheme did provide a measurable disruption at closer ranges, improving as the viewing range increased. However, the effectiveness of any night-vision device falls off markedly as range increases. Dyes used in the camouflage were specifically intended to provide a high IR absorption, matching the IR qualities of the typically vegetation-lacking desert terrain. This camouflage uniform pattern was discontinued after the Gulf War, although it was still listed in AR 670-1 in 2005.

RIGHT: *Coat, Desert Camouflage Pattern: Combat.* The tri-colour desert camouflage was introduced in 1990 as a replacement for the DBDU 'Choc-Chip', which had not been well received. It can be found in cotton and rip-stop fabrics. The scheme was IR-reflective. This Desert Combat Uniform (DCU) is badged to the 10th Mountain Division on the left sleeve with a full-colour US flag on the right sleeve. Above the left breast pocket are badges for helicopter assault and combat infantryman. Collar points bear the insignia of a specialist. This item was manufactured in 1999.

LEFT: Members of the US Air Force 438th Air Expeditionary Group's Honour Guard parade wearing the standard three-colour DCU during a POW/MIA ceremony held in Iraq, 2002. It is the standard army pattern uniform with USAF insignia. US Department of Defense

RIGHT: The subdued desert version of the 10th Mountain Division sleeve insignia, embroidered in brown on a tan base.

The *Blouse, Woodland MARPAT Camouflage, MCCUU,* a component of the Marine Corps Combat Utility Uniform (MCCUU). The MARPAT camouflage schemes incorporate small and discreet EGA (Eagle, Globe, Anchor) devices within the pattern. The EGA is also embroidered on the left breast pocket of USMC 'camies'. This blouse was made in 2004.

Blouse, Desert MARPAT Camouflage, MCCUU. The US Marines have always distanced themselves from the US Army, presenting a high degree of individuality in regard to uniforms and equipment. Their choice of camouflage schemes reinforces this ideal, and, unlike the Army, they have distinct woodland and desert schemes.

LEFT: The US Marines branch of service tape and Eagle, Globe and Anchor logo embroidered on the left breast pocket of a desert MARPAT MCCUU blouse. The 'BOS' (branch of service) tape and 'EGA' are embroidered in black on the woodland uniform.

The label found in USMC-issue garments. It shows the USMC EGA device and states that the item was made expressly for the Department of the Navy, United States Marine Corps.

ABOVE: A US Marine rappels down a cliff during training in 2004. He wears the *Blouse, Desert MARPAT Camouflage, MCCUU*. US Department of Defense

RIGHT: US Navy Petty Officer 1st Class Reynaldo Datu operating in mountainous terrain in eastern Konar Province, Afghanistan. USMC camouflage is worn by naval personnel serving with the Marines, in this instance the woodland MARPAT MCCUU.

RIGHT: Lt. Col. Eric Harris, 101st Airborne Division, wearing the universal camouflage pattern Army Combat Uniform (ACU) during operations in Iraq, 2006. He is carrying a PK-3 SMG.

Coat, Army Combat Uniform (ACU), made up in the Universal Camouflage Pattern (UCP). The camouflage design was adapted from the USMC MARPAT that had preceded it. Black was specifically not included in the scheme as, according to official US Army sources, it was a colour not often found naturally in the environment – apparently they did not appreciate the the visual effect of shadows. This jacket was made in 2005.

Small, concealable IR-reflective patches are fitted on the pocket flaps of the large sleeve pockets, which replaced the hip pockets normally found on uniform jackets. This ACU jacket is badged to a Sergeant first class of the 4th Infantry Division.

This style of jacket was first produced in three-colour desert fabric, as used on the DCU, and trialled with Stryker Brigade units in Iraq during late 2003.

ABOVE: Detail of the 4th Infantry Division patch and the pocket on the left upper sleeve of the ACU jacket. The entire pocket and flap are covered with velcro for the easy placement and removal of insignia. The small nylon tab on the pocket flap covers the IR-reflective patch (visible in the preceding ACU jacket photograph). The right sleeve pocket carries the US flag patch. A variety of unofficial novelty 'theatre' patches can also be found attached to the pockets.

ABOVE: USAF Master Sergeant Randall Williams, photographed during Exercise *Eagle Flag*, held in Alaska during June 2004. MSGT Williams was involved in the testing of new Air Force Battle Dress Uniform types. The blue-dominant camouflage pattern worn here consists of a sky blue base with a sage green and blue overprint with white highlights; it also includes the USAF winged star motive within the print. This colour scheme was not adopted, but the pattern, in a much subdued and digitalized form, and without the winged star, was used on the uniform adopted for service as the ABU. US Department of Defense

ABOVE: The USAF *Coat, Man's Utility, Air Force Camouflage Pattern*, also known as ABU (Airman's Battle Uniform), uses the digital 'Tigerstripe' Air Force camouflage pattern. The prototype of this uniform, trialled during the summer of 2004, used a distinct blue-dominant 'Tigerstripe'. The original pattern was modified to these less vivid hues. Issue of the new uniform began in 2007 and it will be in full service by 2011. This coat was made in 2007.

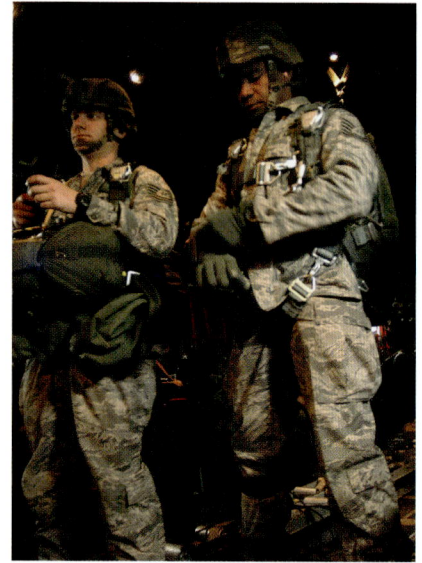

RIGHT: The insignia worn on the ABU are coloured to match the camouflage fabric. Shown here are the 'US AIR FORCE' tab, worn on the left breast, and the rank chevrons for a Staff Sergeant.

ABOVE: US Air Force Tech. Sgts Mark Hawsey and James Turner prepare for a parachute jump with Bulgarian Special Forces during Exercise *Thracian Spring 2008*. Both men wear the ABU camouflage uniform.

ABOVE: In October 2004 the US Navy introduced four different patterns of camouflage uniform for field trials. Shown here, worn by Gunner's Mate 1st Class David K. Bartlett, serving in Kuwait during February 2005, is one of the trials patterns. This concept uniform pattern was one of those that was rejected for issue as the new Navy Working Uniform (NWU).

RIGHT: June 2006, onboard the USS *Constitution*, the US Navy's oldest commissioned warship afloat, two naval officers model the Navy's new digital camouflage BDU-style NWU (based on the USMC MARPAT uniform). This uniform replaced seven previous orders of dress and, although camouflage is not necessary for those working afloat, it does provide a highly serviceable uniform. The camouflage pattern also serves to mask dirt and stains as well as general creasing and wear. Woodland and desert pattern camouflage are still issued to those naval personnel requiring them. US Department of Defense

LEFT: Marines from the 1st Marine Division conduct combat marksmanship proficiency drills during winter mountain operations training at the Mountain Warfare Training Centre, January 2007. They wear the USMC 'Disruptive Overwhite' (snow camouflage) developed by Dr. Timothy R. O'Neill and Guy Cramer. The suit was developed during 2005 and first issued to the USMC in November 2007. US Department of Defense via Guy Cramer/HyperStealth

Yugoslavia

LEFT: This pullover-type smock uses a unique camouflage scheme often called 'mountain camouflage'. It has a 'splatter-spray' pattern that looks as if it has been applied using a poorly adjusted spray gun, and uses a mix of greens and browns on a tan base. There are numerous foliage loops attached to the garment. It is believed that the mountain camouflage was first issued to selected units of the JNA (Jugoslovenska Narodna Armija, or Yugoslav People's Army) during the 1960s.

ABOVE: The M70 'MOL' camouflage over-smock in a scheme often called 'branch pattern'. The smock was issued in a matching camouflage bag with trousers, gloves and face mask. Normally associated with snipers and special forces, the set was made in large numbers and was probably intended for less select issue.

RIGHT: The Serbian double-headed eagle. This historic insignia had been discarded by the Communist regime but was re-introduced to Serbian military forces in 1992. It was worn on the left shoulder of camouflage uniforms and was commonly seen during the Serbian struggle to prevent the break-up of Yugoslavia.

ABOVE: Serbian M89 woodland camouflage shirt. The camouflage scheme uses five colours to produce the disruptive pattern, black, brown, tan and two shades of green. It bears the standard Serbian M92 eagle badge on the upper left sleeve. This shirt was made in 1998.

ABOVE: Serbian soldiers detained by US forces in Kosovo during 1999, are moved to the Serbia-Kosovo border for repatriation to their homeland. Under the requirements of Operation *Joint Guardian*, Serbian forces were required to leave Kosovan territory, or be removed. All wear the M89 camouflage shirt, one bearing the M92 eagle device. The difference in the colour between the camouflage shirts worn by the lead man and the other three is quite marked.

ABOVE RIGHT: Serbian winter jacket showing a variation of the M89 camouflage. The patch above the left breast covers a section of velcro used for the attachment of a rank insignia, Serbian rank was normally displayed in this manner on winter field uniform. This jacket is dated 1998.

RIGHT: Detail showing the velcro section on the left breast of the winter jacket fitted with a rank device. It bears the rank insignia of a Zastavnik I klase (Warrant Officer 1st class, or Sergeant Major).

RIGHT: Serbian special police camouflage jacket showing a further variant of the M89 camouflage. On the left sleeve is a post-1997 'Posebne Jedinice Policije' (PJP, or Serbian Special Police) badge. The jacket was made in 1995 and is cut in a similar pattern to the French F1 uniform jacket.

LEFT: Sleeve badge of the Posebne Jedinice Policije.

LEFT: Serbian police 'urban' 'Tigerstripe'-style camouflage, adopted in 1991. This shirt bears the post 1997 'Policija' badge on the left sleeve. The Posebne Jedinice Milicija (PJM) were renamed Posebne Jedinice Policije (PJP) in 1997.

ABOVE: The early pre-1997 pattern 'Milicija' title worn on the urban camouflage PJM uniform prior to 1997. This design is printed directly on to each sleeve but sewn-on titles are also found.

RIGHT: Detail of the Republic of Serbia 'Policija' badge and rank insignia of a Mladji Vodnik I Klase (Junior Sergeant 1st class).

ABOVE: Serbian Milicija wearing the distinct three-colour urban camouflage used by this unit. The militiaman at left has the 'Milicija' title on his sleeve. The men seem a little uneasy as US troops are searching their accommodation for illegal arms during Operation *Joint Endeavour*, Hajvazi, Bosnia-Herzegovina. The Milicija had a dubious reputation, feared by their enemies, and often by their compatriots too. US Department of Defense

ABOVE LEFT: Serbian 'Lizard' pattern camouflage jacket, one of many variants of camouflage jacket used by Serbia during the civil wars.

ABOVE: Captain Radovan Zoranovic, Commander, 3rd Battalion, 2nd Brigade, Serbian Army (JNA), photographed in January 1996. He wears a jacket using the 'Lizard' pattern camouflage. US Department of Defense

RIGHT: The Albanian nationalist UÇK (KLA, or Kosovo Liberation Army) fought for a Kosovo independent of Serbia. The majority of combatants were Muslim volunteers from other nations. A number of camouflage uniforms were in use with this irregular force, including ex-JNA and Serbian patterns, as well as BW 'Flecktarn'. Turkish pattern camouflage was common and is worn by this UÇK volunteer. It is interesting to compare the camouflage pattern on the upper left thigh of the trousers in this image with the identical print between the two left-hand pockets (as worn) on the Turkish camouflage jacket illustrated in the Turkish section.

Serbian camouflage shirt showing a distinct variation of the 'Lizard' camouflage pattern. A number of variations exist. This shirt was made in 1992.

Glossary

ABDU US Aircrew Battle Dress Uniform, correctly *Coat, Aircrew, Camouflage Pattern; Combat*.

ABL *Armée Belge-Belgisher Leger*. Belgian Army in French-Flemish.

ABU US Airman's Battle Uniform. Correctly *Coat, Man's Utility, Air Force Camouflage Pattern*.

ACU US Army Combat Uniform.

ACU camo US Army Combat Uniform camouflage, correctly 'UCP' camouflage but also know as 'ARPAT', as in ARmy PATtern camouflage.

ANA Afghan National Army.

ARPAT US ARmy PATtern camouflage. Also known as 'ACU', but correctly 'UCP' camouflage.

BGS Bundesgrenzschutz. West German border guard.

Bundesheer Austrian Army.

Burlap *See* 'Hessian'.

BW Bundeswehr. West German armed forces.

CENTRASBAT Central Asian Peacekeeping Battalion. Comprising units from Kazakhistan, Kyrgyzstan and Uzbekistan.

CS95 British. Combat Soldier 95.

DBDU US. Desert Battle Dress Uniform. 'Choc-Chip' camouflage.

DCU US. Tri-colour Desert Combat Uniform.

DDR Deutsche Demokratische Republik – German Democratic Republic, East Germany.

DPM British. Disruptive Pattern Material.

DDPM British. Desert Disruptive Pattern Material.

ECOMOG Economic Community Military Observation Group (Africa).

EGA Eagle/Globe/Anchor device of the USMC.

EOD Explosive Ordnance Disposal.

ERDL US Engineer Research and Development Laboratories.

Hessian A lightweight open-weave fabric typically used in sandbags and camouflage scrim. (US term: 'burlap'.)

HBT Herringbone twill – fabric type.

IFOR Implementation Force. NATO and multinational force in Bosnia-Herzegovina.

IR Infra-red.

ISAF International Security Assistance Force (Afghanistan).

JNA Jugoslovenska Narodna Armija – Yugoslav People's Army.

KFOR Kosovo Force. NATO and multinational force in Kosovo.

KLA Kosovo Liberation Army. Ushtria Çlirimtare e Kosovës (UÇK).

KLMK Russian. *Kamuflirovannyi Letnyi Maskirovochnyi Kombinezon*, or camouflage summer overall.

KZS Russian. *Kostium Zashchitnoi Seti*, or camouflage uniform set.

LBE Load-bearing equipment (webbing or web equipment in British service).

MARPAT US. MARine PATtern camouflage.

MCCUU US. Marine Corps Combat Utility Uniform.

MND-CS Multinational Division – Central-South. Iraq.

NATO North Atlantic Treaty Organization (French – OTAN).

NVA *National Volksarmee*. East German national people's army.

NVG Night-vision goggles.

NWU US Navy Working Uniform.

OD Olive Drab. US Army shade number 7. Green/brown colour used during the Second World War.

OG Olive Green. US Army shade number 107. Green/brown colour introduced during the Korean War.

PJM Posebne Jedinice Milicija – Serbian militia.

PJP Posebne Jedinice Policije – Serbian special police.

PLA People's Liberation Army (China)

PLA(N) People's Liberation Army (Navy). (China.)

RKMC Republic of Korea Marine Corps.

ROK Republic of Korea.

RNoAF Royal Norwegian Air Force, or Luftforsvaret.

RTN Royal Thai Navy.

SFOR Stabilization Force. NATO and multinational force in Bosnia-Herzegovina.

TAZ Swiss. German language *Tarnanzug*, or camouflage uniform.

TAS Swiss. French language *tenue d'assault*, or assault uniform.

UCK Ushtria Çlirimtare e Kosovës (UÇK). KLA, or Kosovo Liberation Army.

UCP US Universal Camouflage Pattern. Also known as 'ACU' and 'ARPAT'.

USAF United States Air Force.

USMC United States Marine Corps.

Volksarmee East German. Peoples Army. NVA, or Nationale Volksarmee.

VSR Vooruzhennye Sili Rossii, or Russian Armed Forces.

Vz Czech language *Vzor*, or model or pattern.

Wz Polish language *Wzor*, or model or pattern.

Select Bibliography and Further Reading

Ord Project Report PR 2003/15 'A Guidebook for the Analysis of Camouflage Data'. DofND. Canada 2003

Ord Project Report PR 2003/4 'The NATO SCI-095 Camouflage Assessment Trial'. DofND. Canada 2003

Army clothing and equipment survey system for the disruptive pattern (CADPAT) user trial. Human Systems Inc. Canada 2000

AR 670-1 Wear and Appearance of Army Uniforms and Insignia. HQ Department of the Army. Washington 2005

The Defence Supply Chain Manual JSP 336 Volume 12 Part 3 Pamphlet 5 Section 4 Combat Soldier 95 (CS 95). MoD 2004

AFI 36-2903 Dress and Personal Appearance of Air Force Personnel. USAF 2006

Dress Instructions. 32 CBG BSL. Canada 2005

Tin Hats to Composite Helmets. M. Brayley. Crowood Press

WWII Tommy in colour photographs. M. Brayley and R. Ingram. Crowood Press

Khaki Drill and Jungle Green. M. Brayley and R. Ingram. Crowood Press

US Marine Corps Uniforms and Equipment in World War 2. Jim Moran. Windrow and Greene 1992

Camouflage Uniforms of Asian and Middle East Armies. J.F. Borsarello and Werner Palinckx. Schiffer 1999

Camouflage Uniforms of European and NATO Armies 1945 to the Present. J.F. Borsarello. Schiffer 2004

Camouflage Uniforms of the Soviet Union and Russia 1937 to the present. Dennis Desmond. Schiffer 1998

Senior Airman Gavalis throws returned uniform items into a fire at Balad Air Base, Iraq. Military uniform and equipment items returned to stores in operational theatres, such as Iraq and Afghanistan, are burned to ensure they are not misappropriated by enemy or insurgent forces. Among the items destined for incineration are DCU and ABU camouflage. Gavalis wears an army UCP coverall.

Index